The
NEW
RESURRECTION

BOOKS

IRH PRESS
New York

ISBN 13: 978-1-942125-64-8
ISBN 10: 1-942125-64-X

Printed in Canada

First Edition

The
NEW
RESURRECTION

My Miraculous Story
of Overcoming
ILLNESS *and* **DEATH**

RYUHO OKAWA

IRH PRESS

CONTENTS

CHAPTER ONE

THE NEW RESURRECTION

1 *Immortal Hero,* Ryuho Okawa's Fight Against a Critical Illness

2 May 14, 2004: the Day of the Heart Attack

3 From a Medical Perspective, I was 'Supposedly Dead'

4 My Conflicts with an Unrealistic Wife and Parenting Five Children

5 From a Miraculous Resurrection to a Great Success

6 "Today is My Whole Life" and "Die for the Truth"

CHAPTER TWO

SERIOUS ILLNESS AND MISSION OF LIFE

Q1 God's Will in the New Resurrection

Q2 Transitioning of the Mission of Life

CHAPTER THREE

A GUIDE FOR THE MIND
- SPECIAL SELECTION -

ADDITIONAL BOOKLET

"TODAY IS MY WHOLE LIFE"
&
"DIE FOR THE TRUTH"

PREFACE

This is a modern day myth.

And it is a book about what I, myself, actually experienced about 15 years ago.

The story will show you how a human, who recognized his death as reality, accomplished true resurrection.

I think this completely goes beyond the common-sense of modern medical science.

Even my former-wife believed that I would be dead on that day, and the doctors also concluded that I was dead.

In a medical magazine, my case has been reported with my gender, age and occupation changed.

On May 14, 2004, I was supposed to have died from a heart attack but what I did was lie down and listen to the CD of *Buddha's Teaching: The Dharma of the Right Mind* for about 30 minutes. Then, I stood up again and went to the hospital for a quick checkup the next morning, but was hospitalized immediately. I was told that if I did not have a heart transplant, I would die that day. However, I was still alive the next morning. So the doctor stated that there was a 90 percent chance I would be dead within the year and they would never let me leave the hospital. 15 years have passed and I, supposedly a ghost by now, am aiming to make my 3,000[th] lecture within this year.[*]

Translator's footnotes

[*] The number of lectures exceeded 3,000 as of the "Spiritual Messages from Sayyid Khomeini [2]" recorded on September 29, 2019.

I do not believe that the same thing will occur to anyone.

This fall on October 18, the live-action movie, *Immortal Hero* will be shown in theatres all across Japan.* It is a story of a hero in solitude. I truly hope that it will give hope and courage to all the people.

Ryuho Okawa
Founder and CEO of Happy Science Group
Aug. 15, 2019

---

* TF: The movie was later decided to be simultaneously released in the U.S. and Canada on October 18, 2019.

Chapter One

THE
NEW RESURRECTION

Lecture given on April 23, 2019
at Happy Science Special Lecture Hall

1

Immortal Hero,
Ryuho Okawa's Fight Against a Critical Illness

The true story that became the basis of the movie

The main theme of this chapter is related to the movie, *Immortal Hero* released in October, 2019 (Executive Producer and original story by Ryuho Okawa).

There are several scenes in the movie which foreshadow the notion of *resurrection*; such the main character, Makoto Mioya, is seen with Tolstoy's novel, *Resurrection* when he fell ill and was hospitalized;

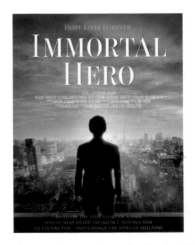

Immortal Hero (Executive Producer and original story by Ryuho Okawa)
Storyline: Makoto Mioya, a highly successful Japanese author and publisher, has a life-threatening, near-death experience. Powerful spiritual beings with whom he has communicated most of his adult life visit Makoto to remind him he has the power within to heal himself. Reborn, Makoto commits his life to sharing the almighty wisdom he receives from the spiritual realm. As doubters, including some of his own family, challenge and question his new-found ardor, Makoto must find a way to connect with his family and to inspire a better world. This movie has currently received 29 awards from 6 countries. Available to watch on VOD (www.immortal-hero.com).

he then publishes a new book called the "The New Resurrection" after recovering from his illness. Also, the theme song titled "New Resurrection" is played toward the end. Since Makoto Mioya is seen writing the book "The New Resurrection" in this movie, I hope to talk about the true story behind this movie.

Already 15 years (2004) have passed since the time I was hospitalized, so my memory of the incident could gradually fade, and the familiar faces of people who were around me at the time have also changed. And now that those who were young back then have become staff or active members of Happy Science, I feel the need to occasionally talk about this story that became a turning point of Happy Science. I also think that there are some things in this story that should be kept as a record, so I wish to do so before I forget.

Even with events that actually happened in my life, how I understand and feel about them can change depending on the current situation I am in. Not only that, how I evaluate individuals who were involved in the event at the time can also change, as my relationship to them has distanced or become closer for various reasons over time.

Along with this movie created 15 years after the incident, I hope to briefly describe to you what the New Resurrection was like, along with my personal comments.

I started a publishing company
As a best-selling author

In 1981, I had my first revelation from heaven. And in 1986, my guiding spirits urged me to resign from my company and become independent. So I made up my mind, and on the day of my 30th birthday, July 7, I handed in my resignation letter.

At first, the company refused to accept my request. Both the sectional and general manager insisted that they could not accept my resignation, so the letter was passed further up the company until it made its way to the vice president. After much disagreement, they finally approved my resignation request.

So, I officially left the company on July 15, as the employment regulation stated that I could only leave one week after submitting the letter. I have previously talked about this in my writings and lectures, but I quit before I was fully prepared to go independent. The movie touches on this part of the story as well.

I also (like Makoto Mioya in the movie) began by publishing books, and gained a fanbase. So I was initially known, not as a religious leader, but as a best-selling author when I established a publishing company.

I did not mind being known as a religious leader from the start, but until Happy Science was officially approved as a religious corporation, I was seen more of as a best-selling author, and that's how I was often treated.

I first established IRH Press Co., Ltd., and used its corporate status to make various contracts. It took about five years for Happy Science to

The main character, Makoto Mioya, is a best-selling author who also manages a publishing company (from the movie *Immortal Hero*).

become recognized as an official religious corporation, but until it did, all contracts were under our incorporated company.

Personally, I saw myself as a religious leader because I was able to receive spiritual messages, but at the same time, I also saw myself as a best-selling author, and so did the majority of the public too. At the time, there was a part of me which thought that it would help to be known as a writer first to gain popularity and attract more people.

In those days, there used to be a list of the highest taxpayers that was publicized annually. So I often applied to the 'Writer' category, but every time, I was put under the 'Other' category instead. Usually, artists and cultural figures are classified into this group. Their reason for placing me in the 'Other' category was because I not only wrote books, but also gave lectures and did other types of activities.

So I was categorized with people like Mr. Ikuo Hirayama, a Japanese style painter who was president of Tokyo University of the Arts, and Mr. Sen Soshitsu, a Japanese tea master of the Urasenke School. I was put in the 'Other' category with such highly esteemed people, so it wasn't bad at all. Before this system became abolished, I was listed side by side with Ms. Hikaru Utada, a blossoming singer at the time, and Mr. Yasushi Akimoto, a lyricist for the Japanese pop group AKB48. I believe my income tax at the time used to be about two to three hundred million dollars.

My books sold by themselves,
And avid readers became my followers

In a way, any new religion tends to have a bad reputation, so Happy Science has been working very hard to transform the impression into a positive one. Since new religions were received quite poorly in Japan after the World War II, it was not easy to promote religious activities. This was true even during the days I was employed.

For this reason, I often received comments from media-personnel and journalists saying how it was wise of me to begin by book writing first; they thought it was a clever strategy to spread the teachings by gaining trust through printed words first.

In the usual case, religions would often already have followers before they publish books, and the books would be bought by them. So from an author's perspective, they would not categorize such a religion to be like them. In my case, however, the books were published before I had any followers. My followers started off as avid readers before becoming a follower, so there was nothing unfair about the way I gained fans and I misled no-one into joining a religion without knowing we are one. The books sold by themselves, and the most avid readers became followers of our religion. That is the truth. Almost all of the people who began by reading my books joined Happy Science. Around the time when the core of Happy Science was built by around 10,000 to 15,000 believers, it was mainly made up by individuals who became avid readers during the first few years after Happy Science began.

My books are certainly influential in that sense. I received a considerable number of letters, too. Due to my prudent and rational nature, I believe I was quite careful and cautious in the beginning.

A movie that illustrates the middle-age burden

I have had several key turning points in my life: the time when I began experiencing spiritual phenomena; the time when I resigned from my job and decided to start Happy Science; the time when Happy Science officially became a religious corporation; the time I got married—just to list a few.

This movie focuses on the main character's internal conflict which arises as he progresses through the various stages of his life, starting from the time when he resigns from his job and becomes a best-selling author; he then marries and builds a family with children; and his work gradually expands. In that sense, this movie is not only an autobiographical episode of a religious leader's life, but also about the weight of responsibilities carried by middle-aged people who are at an age to fill managerial positions. So, I believe many people can empathize with this movie. Perhaps people who have suffered a severe illness in their 40s, who are unsure whether they can return to their job after being discharged from the hospital, may sympathize by watching the movie also.

The movie steps in a little deeper and shows you some of the activities Makoto does after his sense of mission heightens; he begins curing illnesses and giving lectures about the importance of uniting religion for the peace of the world. So in a way, it is like a short summary of my 15 years of life since my New Resurrection.

2

May 14, 2004: the Day of the Heart Attack

My conditions were much worse than seen in the movie

The actual incident occurred on May 14, 2004. When I visited the hospital the following day (Saturday) for a check-up, I was hospitalized unexpectedly. This was how it all began.

In the movie, *Immortal Hero*, the actor added a little drama by acting as if there was some amount of suffering since it would be strange if Makoto appeared as if he had no pain. If he had looked too healthy, there would be no movie, so he did so accordingly.

In reality, the actual condition of my physical body and my symptoms were much worse than how it was portrayed in the movie. As for my physical appearance, I looked far better than how it looked in the movie.

I had not gone for any hospital checkups for several decades. So, when I was asked for my past medical records, I responded that I had none. The doctor was astonished that a 47-year-old had no medical record.

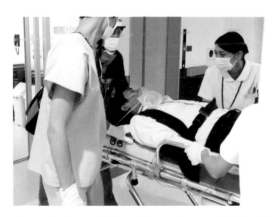

Makoto Mioya is taken to the hospital after suffering a heart attack (from the movie *Immortal Hero*).

He asked, "You must have some sort of medical history," but I told him "I have none. I do not go for checkups because I do not like hospitals." He appeared shocked and may have been wondering why I developed such a critical condition all of a sudden.

Dealing with physical problems using 'the power of my mind'

Perhaps, considering the condition of my physical body at the time, a normal person would have complained or suffered from pain at least several years before developing the critical conditions I was in. I believe so.

In my case, however, since my workload was constantly heavy, I thought it was normal. Even when I felt tightness in my chest, I could not fully recover from fatigue, or felt as if my body was becoming heavier, I thought it was a matter of course. So I was more or less numb to it and thought it was normal. Therefore, when I was at the hospital, the doctor kept saying, "You must be enduring a terrible amount of pain." But what was more painful to me were his words, "You don't need to try so hard." These words hit me really hard.

What he was trying to tell me was to be more like a patient. I strongly believed that my mind is the controller of my body. Even when there were changes or problems to my physical body, I believed strongly that my mind is the controller; my mind is the ruler of my body. The power of my mind was much stronger. When I think back to the past, after I would give a large-scale lecture, I would burn out, be unable to move and become bedridden for about four days. But now, even when I give a lecture at big event halls like Makuhari Messe, Saitama Super Arena, or Tokyo Dome,[*]

---

[*] TF: The capacities of the venues are as follows: 18,000 people at Makuhari Messe, 20,000 people at Saitama Super Arena, and 50,000 people at Tokyo Dome.

I can still give another lecture the following day. What this suggests is that my health condition back then was poorer then how I am now.

I used to think that it was normal to sleep for four days straight as if I'm dead after giving a big lecture, but seeing how fine I am now and how I can get back to work the next day may mean that my health condition was not normal before. I cannot speak for others, but in my case that wasn't normal. I was just used to how I was.

A week before being hospitalized, I walked and inspected the grounds of Nasu Shoja

A week before I was hospitalized, I visited Head Temple Nasu Shoja, which is currently jointly built with Happy Science Academy in Nasu, just before its opening and inspected the place. So I walked the land of what used to be a golf course.

This was in May, so I was wearing a blazer that day. But I remember feeling as though the blazer was about to burst open or it was too tight for my body size. It had me wondering if I "expanded," so I thought I had gotten fat and gained weight. So basically, a week prior to being told that I was a "dead body" by a doctor, I was walking around a hilly site with an area of 250 acres. Although I used a golf cart to move around parts of the place, I was walking around on foot not long before I was called a "dead body," so I probably didn't think that my body was in a bad condition.

My clothes were just feeling really tight. I mean, it felt as though my body was expanding out of my clothes, so I thought I gained some weight. What I didn't know was that there was liquid building up in my body.

The abnormal sensation in my heart
The day before being hospitalized

And on May 14, the day before the hospitalization, I went to Happy Science General Headquarters in the morning. There was some trouble regarding personnel transfers involving the chairperson and chief director of General Headquarters. An argument happened after a new chief director was assigned. Normally, I would not step in, but the argument was slightly escalating, so I headed over to the office on the morning of May 14 to speak with them. But on my car ride home, I felt a sensation I had never felt before. The pain was as if a crow was digging its claws into my heart and clutching it tightly. I probably shouldn't have explained the sensation I had to the doctors like so, but this is what I told them.

At the time, I asked my secretary to play the CD of *Buddha's Teaching: The Dharma of the Right Mind* in the car, and when I got home, I was taken to my room and slept for 30 minutes with *Buddha's Teaching: The Dharma of the Right Mind* playing in the background. Then, I started feeling better like I was 'okay to go.' I was able to walk myself in and out of the dining area at lunch and dinner. But at the same time, there was a part of me who wondered if I should get a physical examination that following Monday since I was coming to the age where I should get regular check-ups. I did not like going to the hospital, but I felt I should go just this once. Most places were closed on weekends, so that is why I thought I should go (on the Monday).

Transferring to a different hospital
That could handle my condition

The following day, on a Saturday morning, while I was walking on the stone steps around my yard however, I somehow felt that I should get a physical exam done as soon as possible. I hadn't experienced any problems with my body, but I just simply felt, "Let's just go for my checkup today instead of Monday," and so I went.

At the hospital, they took various tests, and during the whole process, I was made to walk to each department. When I was taken to the electrocardiogram (EKG) room, they took off my shirt and attached many electrodes to my body. Of course I could not make out what the EKG readings were indicating, but I noticed the doctor's face turning pale blue as he looked at the graphs. Soon after, I was asked if my family was with me, so my wife at the time who was accompanying me was called out of the office to talk privately with the doctor. She was told that my health condition was beyond the capabilities of that hospital and it would be impossible to operate on me there. They urged for me to be taken to a bigger hospital with the appropriate resources. They also mentioned that they will have to use an ambulance when transporting patients from one hospital to another. So someone who had been walking around the hospital to have tests was suddenly thrown into an ambulance, and was transported to another hospital with its siren turned on.

This was my first time experiencing anything like this, and I had only seen such scenes in movies. I was confused why I had to go through all of this, but I was transported to a bigger hospital on the afternoon of the Saturday.

3

From a Medical Perspective,
I was 'Supposedly Dead'

Immobilized heart and lack of blood circulation

There was a renowned cardiologist at this hospital. Once every month, this doctor would give a seminar on a Saturday afternoon, and he was scheduled to give a talk from 2pm to 4pm that very day I was transported. But upon being informed that a man named Ryuho Okawa had been carried in after collapsing, the doctor canceled his talk in haste and came to look at my condition.

The doctor raised the head of my adjustable bed to about halfway, placed what appeared to be a metallic plate behind my back, and took an X-ray of my upper body without taking me to the X-ray room. As he showed me the image, he said, "Do you see the white space covering your heart and lungs? Do you know what that cloudiness indicates? It's all fluid. Your chest from the heart to the lungs is overflowing with fluid." He continued saying, "If you look at the lower part of your heart, you can see that the large amount of liquid has stopped your heart from contracting. When a heart stops contracting, it means there's no blood flowing in. And we all know what that means when blood stops flowing. It means that your condition is equal to a dead person."

I was nodding along as I listened, but I was completely lost about what was going on—I was conscious but apparently my blood wasn't flowing. Right then, another doctor informed us that a catheter was being prepared and he urged me to have an operation done instantly. But I still could not understand what he was saying. I was walking from one department to the next getting my tests done earlier in the day, and now I am suddenly told that, "I am as good as dead." I was totally confused and nothing made sense to me.

The intravenous drip and the urinary catheter

What I was told, that I knew, was to remove much fluid from my body. So the doctors told me to refrain from drinking water. They gave me an intravenous drip (IV) instead through my left arm so that I was not completely dehydrated.

Hospitals tend to immediately resort to giving an IV, and it is quite problematic. Since I was given an IV for a long period, my left arm started weakening, making it harder for me to regain full function of it later on. When they give you an IV, your body creates urine, and since we cannot keep going back and forth to the bathroom, they would put a catheter up the urethra; this was quite a painful experience. The other end of the tube is attached to a urine collection bag which hangs from the bed. The bag will then be replaced once it is full, but the whole system in itself is quite shameful. Hospitals should really think of a better alternative.

Of course, we could not include all the details in the movie, *Immortal Hero*, but there was a part of me who wanted the actor, Mr. Hisaaki Takeuchi, to act out the part where they inserted the urinary catheter as a joke. I hoped they added the scene where Makoto Mioya jumps in pain to show how painful it is in reality. The diameter of the catheter is wider than the urethra, so the pain is unbearable. I suppose, for medical professionals, it's an ideal way for them since the patient's urine will be collected automatically.

As such, I was essentially bedridden and unable to go anywhere with an IV and urinary catheter inserted in me. However, in my mind, I still did not feel that my symptoms were so severe.

To the doctors,
It was impossible for me to have been alive

In any case, after the doctors saw the results from all the tests they did, they said to me, "It is impossible for a normal person to be alive in the condition that you're in." I had no idea what they were saying. That's because I was perfectly fine until the day before. It is true I experienced some sensations that resembled a crow digging its claws into me and clutching my heart, but as soon as I started listening to *Buddha's Teaching: The Dharma of the Right Mind*, the sensation disappeared. So, I thought I was cured.

In that regard, I was not sure if this was caused by actual issues in my physical heart or by spiritual matters. The reason I say this is the chairperson at the time, who was incumbent only for a short period, was a crow-like goblin in a spiritual sense. So during the transfer after his short incumbency, I fought against him (spiritually).* While I struggled to distinguish the issue as a spiritual one or a medical one, the doctors were confident that the sensation of 'claws digging into my heart and clutching it tightly' was due to a myocardial infarction. They also believed I should have been dead when I was walking around my garden on the previous day.

---

* TF: When people continue to possess strong, hostile emotions, such as feeling anger or holding a grudge toward someone specific, his or her negative energy can connect with their own guardian spirit and travel to the person and cause trouble in their lives. This is called *ikiryo*, or the "spirits of the living." The spiritual conflict mentioned here is referring to the attack from the *ikiryo* with an appearance of a Crow-like Goblin.

Such assumptions I think are actually hard to believe. The doctors persistently said to me, "You had a heart attack, so it's impossible for you to be alive today." Even when they told me that, I couldn't understand since I walked to the dining room by myself to have lunch and dinner after I had the sensation; medically speaking, I should have collapsed and died right then.

In the movie *Immortal Hero*, however, this part is portrayed in a way that the story is convincing to the audience, so I was not able to accurately illustrate the situation exactly how it was.

Myocardial infarction, heart failure, Pulmonary edema, silent angina pectoris...

Either way, that's how I became hospitalized. But the one moment that made me think I might really be ill was when I was helped into a wheel chair and I wheeled myself to the wheel-chair accessible restroom. While I was in the toilet, I felt something very different and a little pain that it made me think, "Wait a minute, maybe there is something wrong with me." That was the lowest point of my day.

Just like how it was depicted in the movie, in the evening of the same day, the doctors informed my family to prepare for the worst because it was unlikely for me to make it through the night.

Even the doctors seemed confused. They were saying all sorts of things. I understood what a myocardial infarction or heart attack was, but they mentioned a list of unfamiliar medical terms, including heart failure and pulmonary edema. They explained that I had a heart failure since my heart wasn't contracting, and pulmonary edema because my lungs were filled with water. On top of that, I was also diagnosed with angina pectoris but a 'silent' angina pectoris.

I presume they called it 'silent' angina pectoris because I kept on insisting that I experienced no pain. But it made me wonder if 'having no pain' is even a symptom that can be called an illness. If that's the case, a 'silent' heart attack may exist, but that's what the doctor diagnosed me as having. They looked puzzled themselves. The data may have suggested that my symptoms were something similar to it, but it is likely that they had existed from years ago and I had been working despite it all.

If a normal person had been giving as many lectures as I have, it would not be a surprise if the person had died over and over. Regardless of my physical condition, I continued to live.

The people around me were shocked
When I ate or read books in my hospital bed

When I was admitted to the hospital, they measured my weight, but since I was not allowed to walk, they hung me up to weigh me. Like the old-time measuring scale, they put a vinyl sheet on me and lifted me up to an elevated position and checked my weight. I remember being suspended over my bed, as if I were a tuna fish being weighed.

As it turns out, I was a "big catch" of 161 pounds, so the doctors urged that I lose at least 11 to 13 pounds. I actually managed to lower my weight to less than 145.5 pounds by the time I was discharged from the hospital. I really focused on losing my weight.

Strangely enough, the meals at the hospital seemed better than what was served at my house—what I mean is the portions were much bigger at the hospital. Since I usually did not eat as much at home, I was astonished at the portions of the hospital meals. It made me worried that by eating it all, my weight might increase. That's how much there was.

Like so, the doctors and I had widely differing opinions. We simply knew that there was something wrong (with my body).

By then, I had already received messages from the guiding spirits of Jesus Christ and Edgar Cayce who both told me that I would leave the hospital in a week to ten days' time. With that in mind, I was lightheartedly preparing my next project while I was still hospitalized. But the people around me were the exact opposite. They looked at me as if I was some kind of ghost, and was wondering what on earth was happening to me.

For example, as a rule, dinner would be brought to any patient that is hospitalized, at an early hour. Whenever the nurse would bring my dinner to my bed at around 5pm, I would sit upright on my bed and start eating. But even the nurse who delivered the meal to me would be surprised to see me eat. Of course she brought the food to me expecting me to eat it, but her expression was enough for me to sense her astonishment as to why I could eat at all. I would even be reading paperback books and studying books on Buddhism, so everyone seemed to be surprised by that as well.

My former wife repeatedly said to me, "You are a dead man"

Then at around six o'clock in the evening, my family visited me to say their last goodbyes. I'll only say a little as it could spoil the movie, but that appeared to have been their main reason.

My wife at the time, Kyoko, was an honest person. Even when she was asked not to tell anyone what she was told, she would still say it out loud. When I included lines of what she said in the movie (script), the filmmakers said, "No way, this can't be true."

The movie contains many lines which accurately reflect what was said, but everyone would say, "No person would ever say such things. More so a wife would not talk like this. Neither would doctors."

The medical experts and filmmakers (who read the script) could not believe it, and tried to change the lines, but I insisted that those were the exact words, and that I heard them many times with my own ears. My eldest daughter, Sayaka Okawa, who was in charge of the script, summed it up nicely.

It is true that no one would usually say, "You are a dead man" to someone who's eating a meal. But those were the words I was repeatedly told and I'm not the only one who heard this.

I refused to have an organ transplant since brain death is not death

What's more, I was even told, "You won't survive much longer. Your only option is to have an organ transplant." It was just around this time that I heard the news of a child who was gathering funds to have a heart transplant. The child was trying to make 800,000 dollars to cover the cost to have it done in the United States, but he passed away during the process.

At this point, the Japanese Diet had already passed the Organ Transplant Law (enacted in 1997) which ruled brain death as a sign of legal death only in regards to an organ transplant. Brain death is simply death based on materialistic judgments, but when a doctor confirms a brain death, the patient would be considered dead and his or her organs can be removed for transplantation.

What they are trying to do is to determine the time of death of a patient who is already about to die as quickly as they can. They want to remove and transplant the organs while they are still fresh to increase the survival rate of the person receiving the transplant. So, even if the heart is still moving in one way or another, if no brainwaves are detected or if there is hardly any activity in the brain, the doctors can approve brain death based on the Organ Transplant Law.

Happy Science, however, from a religious standpoint, opposes the law by explaining that, "The soul does not leave the body while the heart is still moving. So humans are not dead at that point."

Therefore, when the doctor told me, "Your examination shows a variety of symptoms. But since the image shows that your heart has expanded, you must have dilated cardiomyopathy. So you can only survive by having an organ transplant," I remember answering, "No, Happy Science is against organ transplants. It would create greater problems to me if you gave me one."

The lonely night, even when I knew
I won't die since no spirit came to "pick me up"

At this point, most of the people around me all believed that I would not make it through the night. I won't go into detail since it may spoil the movie, but there is a scene where my family brings in a family photo and leaves it on the table in my hospital room.

In reality, my ex-wife had placed the photo on my overbed table. When she left it there, I soon realized that she was also thinking that I was going to die. It said a lot. There were also three executives of Happy Science Religious Affairs Headquarters, one of whom was a doctor, that kindly came to say their goodbyes. Only the three of them came because it was not realistic for all Happy Science staff to attend.

But my brain was sharp and my vision was clear, and I was even able to see that the three of them were under bad spiritual influence, so I remember sending them home. I told them, "You are all spiritually disturbed. You are possessed by evil spirits, so you shouldn't be visiting me. You could worsen my condition, so don't visit me anymore."

I still clearly remember how they, the Chief Secretary of Religious Affairs Headquarters, one other person, and a doctor, were all under spiritual influence.

Even so, I couldn't help but feel lonely at night. I would think, "What if what I'm thinking is wrong." Yet, the guiding spirits had already clearly told me, "You will be discharged," and I knew that if a person like me was to die, (the spirits of) my family members or ancestors would have come to greet me. But not a single person had come, so I was convinced that I was not going to die.

A year before this incident (2003), my father (Saburo Yoshikawa, Honorary Advisor of Happy Science), had passed away, and so had my aunt (Shizuko Nakagawa, a novelist) and older brother (religious name, Makoto Tomiyama) already a while back; all of them should have come to greet me. But because none of my close family members came to pick me up, I knew that it wasn't the time for me to die.

Even when I knew this, when day would turn to night, I would find it difficult to sleep. I would wake up often in the middle of the night.

A thankful nurse and
The remarkable response of a nurse

On the bright side, there was a night shift nurse who came on duty one night whom I felt knew what was in my mind. I sensed some light from her, so she was angel-like, or perhaps she was receiving inspiration from a guiding spirit. She very confidently said to me, "I won't let you die." I was very thankful that there was someone who would say something completely the opposite from the doctors.

Yet, during the night, I would have a difficult time going to sleep as my mind would think of many past events, thoughts and feelings. The lyrics of the main theme song of this movie describe my thoughts and feelings I had at the time.

Fortunately, I did not die and woke up still alive the next morning. So I requested a notepad and a pen from the morning shift nurse and wrote down specific work instructions for the chairperson of Happy Science as well as my thoughts to my family. Much like the previous day, the nurse from whom I asked for the notepad and pen was shocked by my request, and further shaken by the sight of me writing something on the paper. Her response was so remarkable that I almost told her to stop looking so shocked and be happy that I am alive. But I'm sure the situation was something unbelievable to her.

4

My Conflicts with an Unrealistic Wife and Parenting Five Children

The movie's accurate interpretation of the light approach I took toward marriage

Through this incident, I remember it made me feel very thankful to have a family. My former wife used to bring me various things and a change of clothes twice every day.

The movie, *Immortal Hero*, illustrates my marriage scene with a slight humor, but in actuality, unlike any normal person, my marriage did not develop from a romantic relationship. I mean, when I quit my company and became independent, I already knew the kind of person I was, the kind of life I would be living, and felt I didn't need to marry. I was planning to do everything by myself without causing problems to anyone, so marriage didn't cross my mind. I would only think about marriage if my partner were to understand the risks of being with me and still wanted to marry me regardless. So in this sense, this movie portrayed my marriage in a comical manner with a slightly different setting to what happened in reality, but it accurately depicts how lightly and easily I decided on my marriage.

I simply was not thinking about getting married, and would only consider it if there was someone who wanted to marry me and was willing to sacrifice and offer her life to the marriage. Even if I did marry, there was also a part of me that could not promise a typical future.

A fortune-teller once told me when I was young that I will not be able to decide who I marry and that the woman will decide for me; and the prediction came true. So out of the ordinary in this world, I actually got engaged over a cup of coffee.

The consequences of my marriage to a truly unrealistic person

While there were certain parts of my actual experiences that were left out of the movie, *Immortal Hero* still contains many of the unrealistic instances I experienced. The unrealistic situation in the movie was the reality in itself that I experienced, and much like the many unrealistic characters who appeared in the movie, my family and the people I met in real life were also truly unrealistic.

The person who became my wife was a truly unrealistic person. According to the movie, we supposedly met at a marriage consultation agency, but in reality, that's not how we met. On our first date, I was actually constrained into an engagement over a cup of coffee after what truly felt more like a prosecutorial investigation. She answered with a straight "No" when I asked if she wanted a coffee refill, and appeared as though all she wanted was the conclusion. She wouldn't put down her guard, and was making sure I take full responsibility for initiating the date. I wasn't even allowed to go to the restroom.

This "investigation" continued for five hours at the café, and as soon as I started talking about marriage, she said "Yes" and 'the prosecutor' finally loosened up. She then reached into her bag and pulled out a white piece of paper and said, "I would like you to fill out this resume." The form asked for my income, age, blood type, height, weight, family makeup, etc., which reminded me of a resume template that people use when they apply for jobs. This was something she brought with her on our first date.

I was surprised there were such people in the world; it was unbelievable, but I would say that she was very work efficient. Such a work efficient person accompanied me while I was sick at the hospital, so perhaps she naturally wanted to send me off into the other world more efficiently.

In any case, when I saw the resume and asked her why I should fill it out, she said, "It's because I need to send it to my parents." She was very efficient like this. Like so, I had an 'unrealistic marriage' and an 'unrealistic near-death experience' once in my life.

My former wife had "religious faith," "Academic faith," and "medical faith"

Moreover, my ex-wife seemed to have taken the doctor's words very seriously. Her family in Akita Prefecture ran an obstetrics and gynecology clinic which takes inpatients, so she also had "medical faith."

When we first got married, we somehow managed to get along with each other despite some conflicts here and there. But as Happy Science grew, the contradictions in our faith began to show. My wife at the time had not only a firm "religious faith," but also "academic faith" and "medical faith." These three were firmly implanted in her.

It is true that new religions were frowned upon after the World War II in Japan, so people could not be open about their faith at the time. As for my marriage, my former wife's parents agreed to take me because my educational background and income were good, and they judged that I'm not a crazy person since I've had a career working at a trading company in New York and was appreciated in a worldly aspect.

To add to that, since my ex-wife decided to get married as she was about to graduate from university, her friends and the professor in her seminar were surprised at how early she was making the commitment. She was actually frustrated at her friends' proclamations that she would never be able to marry, so she was very keen on being the first one to do so. Back then, it was difficult for a professor to publish a book. So when she informed her professor about her marriage and showed him my 'resume,' he saw that I was a CEO of a publishing company. It seemed to have caught his attention that he eagerly asked whether I could help him publish a book.

Even her friends seemed to suggest that I was not a regular religious leader, having graduated from the University of Tokyo, written books, and lived in New York. In this way, she probably had three faiths: religious faith, academic faith, and medical faith.

The struggle of raising five children
To become religious leaders

My ex-wife and I still had some minor misunderstandings when Happy Science first started, but I was just about managing to keep everything balanced and together. But as the organization grew and I had all five of my children, my family responsibilities started weighing down on me.

I don't know how I managed to cope up until the fourth child. I was like an unsinkable aircraft carrier, but as our fifth child came, my family responsibilities became heavier, that I couldn't work as freely as before.

The biggest problem was raising my eldest son. About half of the worries and concerns I had for my children were of him. One of the reasons is because he had hyperactive tendencies. But my wife at the time was convinced it was a learning disability.

For some reason, most of my children struggled with arithmetic and mathematics, so they would often miscalculate or forget the formulas. Perhaps because I was a religious leader, my children naturally focused their efforts more on language and literature. They may have taken all the mastering of basic addition and subtraction, that are a prerequisite to function adequately at a workplace, too lightly as they were able read books. But due to such reasons, I felt they were weak at logical reasoning.

What's more, my former wife wasn't sure how to raise the children to become religious leaders. Much like raising a successor to a company, she probably thought that it would be enough for them to focus on applying for a good middle school and taking the fast-track course to becoming elites. Again, this is another area that created confusion in our lives.

The mind is essentially what's important in religion, so there is great meaning in being able to train the mind, polish the mind and refine the mind to being as clean as a mirror as well as being able to discover the wrong in other people's minds. But perhaps my ex-wife did not quite understand the importance of it well. If anything, she seemed to have been more concerned about worldly matters instead.

Then in 2001, my eldest son failed miserably in his middle school entrance exam and ended up going to his third or fourth choice as a result, and in 2003, my eldest daughter had her entrance exam as well. When my children were born, I did not think about all the entrance exams that were waiting in the future. It did not cross my mind at the time and I just assumed that once the children were born, all I needed to do was raise them; but a harsh reality waited for me instead. Since my children were two years apart, it meant that the entrance exams were to come every two years.

I was already finding it quite difficult to work while my children were little, but there was something even more challenging about having to deal with entrance exams every two years for five children.

In this way, my family situation was very difficult at the time. It felt quite unbearable, and I wondered how a father can find time to work at the same time. The movie briefly illustrates this part of my life.

My eldest son applied for school in 2001, my eldest daughter in 2003, and with an extra one year interval, my second son applied in 2006, my third son in 2008, and my second daughter in 2010. When my youngest was born in 1997, I thought that the hard part was over, but then the entrance exams started in 2001. I was actually anxious and worried feeling as if this was the end of me if it continued. I had quite a lot happening along these lines which caused a lot of conflicts, so I may have over-stretched myself back then.

I'm sure Happy Science members are also experiencing a lot of hardships balancing both their family life with their activities at Happy Science.

5

From a Miraculous Resurrection to a Great Success

Walking 1,900 miles and losing weight
After my discharge from the hospital

When I was hospitalized in 2004, the doctors spoke to me as if I was already dead. They said to me, "You will die today," "You will die tomorrow," or "You will definitely die within the year." They even said, "Nobody in your condition has lived more than five years," "No matter how you look at it, you will not live for 10 years." These are some of the things they told me.

After being moved to a room on the fourth floor of the hospital, I was even told, "We will not allow you to step out of the fourth floor for the rest of your life." What they meant was they needed to keep an eye on me. They must have anticipated that I would be pressured to work by a large number of Happy Science staff if I were to be discharged. If that happened, I would be killed from overwork, so they were resolute on not letting me leave the hospital. But even if I survived, it

Makoto Mioya tells the doctor that he aims to cure his illness with the power of his mind (from the movie *Immortal Hero*).

would cause problems if I were to live the rest of my life in a hospital. In any case, the hospital strongly prohibited work-related visitors since it would lead to work, and only allowed family to visit. This was the hospital's fundamental policy for me.

Once I was discharged, I felt the need to train my body again, so I started losing weight by walking regularly. I managed to drop over 22 pounds by walking a total distance of about 1,900 miles, which is roughly the span of the Japanese archipelago.

I publicized this story in the winter of 2008 (February, 2), when I gave an English lecture called "About *An Unshakable Mind*." Shio Okawa, my current wife and Aide to Master & CEO said, "I watched the lecture in my final year at Waseda University. Until then, I didn't know you had fallen ill." This was in 2008, so four years had passed since the incident.

To tell the truth, I kept quiet about the experience until I gave that lecture, and only a few people knew about it even at our General Headquarters. All the staff at Religious Affairs Headquarters were of course told about it, but they were very close-mouthed and they prevented the news from spreading. So there were only four people who knew at the General Headquarters.

For example, the Director General of the Media and Arts Projects Division who were in charge of producing *Immortal Hero* (at the time of this lecture) exclaimed, "Master Okawa's illness? I don't know what you are talking about. I've been here (as part of Happy Science) for 30 years, and I've never heard of such a thing. That can't be true." In terms of phrases such as, "You are a dead man" and "This is a battle between medicine and a new religion!" that comes up many times in the movie, the staff would say, "I haven't heard of such a thing. These phrases are too unrealistic to have actually happened." The news was kept a total secret.

As a result, they attempted to change the plot so it was in line with the standards of worldly medical knowledge and tried to make it as though I had a near-death experience. I explained to them that I did not have a near-death experience and that I was told I was already dead. And yet they struggled to accept the story as it is, so it was challenging making this movie. Other people also responded in a similar way.

I also experienced the following situation. Around 2007, when I felt I was recovered enough from the illness, I began focusing more on lecturing again. This episode happened when I delivered a lecture at Tokyo Shoshinkan, one of the main temples at Happy Science, to kick start my missionary tours in Japan.

At the lecture, Mr. Hajime Kuki, who was at the time the Chief Secretary of Religious Affairs Headquarters, brought a chair from the back for me, so I sat down. Then, two former secretaries who are now executives, Ms. Mihoshi Aizen and Ms. Noriko Tatsunokuchi, came to me upon seeing this and said, "Master Okawa, it is uncool to sit on a chair when you give a lecture at a place like Tokyo Shoshinkan. Please stand up!" They actually used the word 'uncool.'

Since they were urging me to stand as if I were a knocked-down boxer taking the count, I told them, "OK. I will stand from the next lecture." They said so because they actually had no idea I was ill at that point, so Mr. Kuki was criticized for bringing out the chair. I attempted to give the next lecture standing and discovered it was not bad at all. I realized that anything is possible if you give it a try. This was in 2007.

The decision I made after the doctor told me
That I only have 5 to 10 years to live

At the time, I was not sure if I was going to die within 5 or 10 years like the doctor told me, but there was one thing I decided; "If it really is my last, then I shall live my life with no regrets."

Around that time, I unexpectedly decided to stop by Osaka Central Branch while I was out visiting the Kansai area. While I was talking with three to four staff members at the branch, the news of my presence at the branch seemed to have spread like wildfire amongst the branch members. So when I stepped out after about an hour, I was met by about 200 people outside.

A large group of female followers surrounded me and I was pushed and shoved in the crowd. I felt sorry that I could not do much for them when they traveled all the way to see me, so I offered that they can touch me anywhere they want. I remember having my hems and shirt tugged at and being touched all over. I still remember this episode.

From this experience, I strongly sensed that the people were yearning for more lectures, and realized I needed to start giving lectures again. So from the end of June in 2007, I began doing missionary tours in Japan. Perhaps my actions like these made my wife at the time think I was insane.

I've given over 2,000 lectures and
Established a school and a political party

It was around this time that my ex-wife, convinced that I would be dying soon, began her preparations to be the next successor of Happy Science. That is to change the faith of Happy Science to that of faith in Monju.

This was because Happy Science referred to Akita Prefecture, which is her home town, as "Jun-Seichi, Akita," meaning 'Semi-holy land, Akita,' and built a Monju Temple (currently Akita Shinkoukan) there.

Seeing how I started to speak of going on missionary tours across Japan, perhaps in her eyes, I had finally lost it and was preparing to die as a kamikaze unit. What's more, even though I had no plans for it at that point, I started going on overseas missionary tours in November of 2007 starting with an English lecture in Hawaii.

There may have been a part of me that became desperate. It is true that I felt like I might as well do all I can, and die like a samurai of the sky, and perish with the wind. At the very least, I would have looked as if I had gone crazy to a person who had witnessed when I was on the verge of death from an illness.

To add further, right after I fell ill, I had written nine years' worth of opening messages, 'A Guide for the Mind,' (refer to Chapter 3) for our monthly magazine. Even if I were to die along the way, I thought Happy Science could still maintain its followers while my words continued to appear on the monthly magazine. Yet, since I suddenly started a missionary tour, I may have appeared like I had lost my mind.

Perhaps I should have limited my activities to simply going on domestic and overseas missionary tours only, but by 2010, I had established Happy Science Academy Junior and Senior High School in Nasu, and by 2013, the Kansai School was completed. On top of that, I also established the political party, Happiness Realization Party in 2009, by which I could have appeared to have fallen into a state of confusion. My ex-wife and I started to grow apart in the process. She eventually started living alone in a home built near the Master's Holy Temple for about two to three years. She may have had some pressure from my disciples in making this decision.

Even then, she still undertook the role of becoming the party leader of the Happiness Realization when we first started living apart. But it wasn't long until she abandoned her responsibilities and left me to pick up after her.

In her eyes, I may have seemed like I was preparing to die like a true hero, much like the pilot in the movie *The Eternal Zero* where the driver dives and crashes into an aircraft carrier on a bomb-filled zero fighter plane. Naturally, anyone would have seen it that way.

I believe I had given about 900 lectures and published 300 books before I fell seriously ill in 2004. Since then, I have given over 2,000 lectures, and by the end of 2019, I will have given 3,000 lectures. Moreover, I have also given 130* or so English lectures, and continued to carry out a multitude of other projects.

In short, a man who was told, "You are a dead man" later published over 2,200 books, including translations. The impossible happened, and that is for sure.

---

* TF: As of December, 2019, the number of English lectures has exceeded 150.

6

"Today is My Whole Life" and "Die for the Truth"

Because I still have a mission, I will keep going

Already 15 years have passed since I should have left this life. But I am still alive here today, so I truly feel sorry. I lived each day thinking I may die anytime soon, but I am still here today. Surprisingly, we don't die so easily. I thought I wouldn't live for too long, so I tried accomplishing something every day and lived thinking, "Today is my whole life." And when I realized, the number of my lectures and books just kept increasing to this many.

I already had my 60th birthday, and outlived Nichiren and Kukai. My life would have been over if I were either of them, but for now, my 'diesel engine' is still going strong.

Shakyamuni Buddha is said to have lived to about 80 years of age, so when I first started Happy Science at age 30, I promised to continue working for another 50 years. The reason I have been able to pick up and continue my work after having died once is probably because I have missions that are yet unaccomplished. I thought I had finished teaching the laws at the time. But I find myself quite surprised to find that there is still more and more. I have also started various new projects, like establishing a university, producing movies, and composing songs. I truly feel that humans have so much potential. I personally feel that there is still more and more room for growth at this point.

Truly understanding the meaning of "Today is my whole life" and "Die for the Truth"

Some of you already know what I spoke about in this lecture. Whether you read this lecture before you have watched the movie, *Immortal Hero*, I don't know. But here, I have summarized the events that actually happened to me. This is my New Resurrection.

After I experienced death at first hand, and the feelings of "I may die tomorrow or within the year," the true meanings of "Today is my whole life" and "Die for the Truth" seeped deep into my soul.

For example, when I went to Brazil on a missionary tour, out of ignorance and my preconceived image of Brazilian cities located along the Amazon River, I genuinely imagined that I would be touring and giving lectures along the Amazon River and could die along the way.

But when I actually got to São Paulo, I was surprised to see helicopters transporting cash across the city. Money is transported between bank buildings by helicopter because there is a chance of encountering a robbery on the streets. After seeing this, it made me think that maybe Brazil could be more advanced than Japan. I had minor misunderstandings of Brazil in such ways, but because Brazil had more urban districts than expected, I never actually made it to the Amazon River.

I was even able to go on a missionary tour in Africa as well, so there were many good things that have happened after my illness.

This concludes the brief explanation of the before and after of my New Resurrection.

Chapter Two

SERIOUS ILLNESS AND MISSION OF LIFE

Lecture given on April 23, 2019
at Happy Science Special Lecture Hall

Q1 God's Will in the New Resurrection

Questioner A

Thank you very much for today's lecture Master Okawa. You mentioned that when you experienced the New Resurrection, your family and other people like your secretaries were with you at the time. It seemed like the closer some of the people were to you, the more they were unable to understand the true meaning behind this historical happening. They would simply consider it as a normal illness or as part of an everyday situation.

I would appreciate it if you could teach us the important mindset we should have so that we do not overlook God's Will in the New Resurrection phenomenon.

Curing illness

What it means is I can now cure illness. I can cure illness because I had a serious illness. This is the main point.

Some kind of faith in medicine is becoming more and more established today, while religion has greatly detached from medicine. In the past, religions were greatly involved in curing illnesses and new religions were the same as well. But Western medicine started to win as people began thinking that the chance of recovering at a hospital was higher and more effective. When medicine is regarded as a part of science, both the advancement of science and the decline of magic seems to occur together at the same time.

This has created a world where people think that new religions do not cure illness, and it put me in a difficult position. That is why I did not actively engage in curing illness until then.

As a matter of fact, in 1992, Mr. Susumu Shimazono, an Associate Professor of Religion at the University of Tokyo at the time, once wrote about Happy Science; he said something like, "A religion that does not heal illness," in one of the volumes of the Iwanami Booklet series published by Iwanami Shoten.

This is because the professor believed the following: "From the past, the fundamental role of religion has been to resolve poverty, illness, and conflict. In terms of poverty and illness, religion should help cure people who have fallen ill because of poverty. As for conflict, religion should help settle family conflicts. In this way, religion is supposed to deal with issues involving poverty, illness, and conflict. However, new religions that are established in this affluent modern society no longer talk about it. And we now have another religion that teaches about how to achieve success through self-help, like those popular in the United States." Like so, he described Happy Science as one of the religions of this affluent time.

I remember Mr. Shoichi Watanabe (professor emeritus of Sophia University) also once told me that it is rare to see a religion that states that they do not cure illness.

"Medical Faith"
Interfered with curing illness

One of the reasons (why I did not actively cure illnesses) was because my former wife was the daughter of a doctor, so she had medical faith.

To tell the truth, as Happy Science grew, the revenue of her parent's hospital started to decrease significantly. They run an obstetrics and gynecology clinic. But after I taught in my lectures that the souls of an aborted baby are not able to return to heaven, the number of women going for an abortion in their clinic decreased, and that affected their income. I felt sorry for them, but that was what happened.

One other reason was because I was able to think from a legal stand point since I studied law in university. So some kind of mental constraint made me think that only medical professionals who are certified by law or licensed should be legally allowed to cure people, and so I should not talk about curing illness.

Seicho-no-Ie is a religion which started their activities in 1930, and they had been advertising their book, *Seimei-no-Jissou* from before World War II. I recall their advert in the newspaper which read something like, "You can cure your illness just by reading our books." If anyone posted an advert with such a slogan today, they will either be prosecuted for fraud or for violating the Medical Practitioner's Act in Japan. The conditions today are greatly different from before. In other words, curing illness is essentially a part of religious activities, but it was done underground, not on the surface-level, and practiced only inside the religious organization.

Take Christianity, a world religion for example. There is only less than 100 cases that the Vatican has recognized as a true healing miracle that has happened at the Lourdes.

As we can see in movies involving exorcists, the only people the Vatican-approved exorcists can exorcise are people who have already been diagnosed at the hospital. If the illness needs hospital treatment or, in other words, the hospital decides that the patient has a psychological or mental illness that will involve taking medication and hospitalization, an exorcism cannot be performed. They cannot perform exorcism if there is no evidence showing that the person is actually spiritually possessed. They reluctantly accept only a very small number of people they could actually see doing something abnormal, such as "guessing right what is inside a bag" or some paranormal activities. We can see that this is the case from various movies.

The Roman Catholic Church is said to receive over 500,000 requests for an exorcism every year, but only a handful appears to be actually answered. Even if they do get chosen, most of the time, it is likely to be ineffective. In reality, they are probably much weaker (than the demons) and are driven into a corner.

The question is, can an individual who has a rational mind and has taken modern-day education really cure illnesses of people in such a state. This was very difficult to overcome, but after my New Resurrection, I have become able to cure many kinds of illness.

Miracles that are happening one after another After my New Resurrection

Even I couldn't believe it myself; I understood when I heard about people being cured from an illness after watching a Happy Science movie, but recently, I hear that people are recovering just by receiving a Happy Science flier.

So what do you think? It's hard to say because this depends on the level of faith of individuals. And I wonder, "Can someone truly be cured just by receiving a flier?" But what this might be suggesting is that we have entered into "the world of the True Pure Land Buddhism."

Originally, Pure Land Buddhism had their followers chant "Namo Amitabha Buddha" one million times to be saved. The number of recitations required for salvation was eventually decreased to 10 times, then to once, and was reduced even further to the point where you would already be saved when you believe that Amitabha Buddha will come to save you.

If the practice of Happy Science is going through a similar evolution, then I believe it can happen. We have seen people who have recovered from taking Happy Science ritual prayers, watching our movies, reading my books, watching my lecture DVDs, listening to my lecture CDs, and reciting *Buddha's Teaching: The Dharma of the Right Mind*. So I guess it can happen by being introduced to Happy Science by a flier.

The more our religious organization gains spiritual power like a magnet, I believe that some people can become spiritually connected (to the heavenly world) just by having those chances. For example, it may happen when someone who had been strongly against Happy Science— even against their own family member who are our believers—to suddenly have God's light enter them the moment they accept Happy Science. It can happen.

The bigger and stronger the spiritual power of our organization becomes, the more of such phenomena are likely to occur. For example, we have been seeing gold powder at my lectures, and it is becoming a normal occurrence. It appeared in Taiwan when I gave a Japanese lecture there; even when Sayaka Okawa, Chief of CEO's Office, and Shio Okawa, Aide to Master & CEO, gave a lecture on the picture books they had written, gold powder was seen around the children in the audience.

On another occasion, when my family and I were talking about the gold powder which appeared on a previous day, it appeared on my grandchild's head. The gold powder phenomenon is becoming a common occurrence. So when you talk about faith, unless you actually experience such kind of phenomena yourself, it won't deepen at all.

The same is true for spiritual messages. I already had faith in God and Buddha since I was a child, and I believed that the afterlife, spirits, and paranormal phenomena existed. However, I noticed a tremendous difference before and after I actually started to receive direct messages from spirits.

Even if I say that they are direct messages from spirits, I am sure there are many fake ones out in the world. That is why I published a large number of spiritual message books. When you listen to the recordings of the spiritual messages, you might feel that the voices are the same as they are spoken through me. But by transcribing them and putting them into text, people have been able to identity the difference in the way each spirit speaks. They could see their unique characters, and really tell that they are the spirits of the person they said they were. These experiences have certainly helped deepen faith greatly.

We started to strengthen what
Other religions were already doing

In this way, my New Resurrection was when I took another leap from the time I attained the ability to receive spiritual messages. As Happy Science started curing illness, which is what other older traditional or newer religions were already doing, we were able to strengthen what we didn't focus on and make it stronger.

Until this point, our activities were focused mainly on spreading our books that taught about how to improve one's mind to live an honest and sincere life. From such a level, Happy Science took a significant step forward into doing what religions would usually do and making it our standard. This was a great development.

Perhaps before this leap, many people thought that Happy Science was an organization for people to become enlightened. When Happy Science first began, many of our staff was bureaucrats or business elites that wore suits to work. Among them were those who believed that it was better for us to take a more rational approach.

When we were deciding if we should register our organization as a religious corporation or not, there was disagreement between the executives at the time. Some of them said, "People dislike religion, so we should apply for a corporation aggregate instead."

If we had registered under a corporation aggregate, the individuals in the group would not be "employees," but "members" who are a part of this corporation aggregate, so we would not have been considered a religion. In this way, there were people who actually preferred Happy Science to be "Corporation Aggregate Happy Science" because a religious corporation sounded uncool to them.

Compared to those days, it is clear that the faith of our members have evolved and developed.

Advanced medicine vs. a new religion

In the movie *Immortal Hero*, Makoto Mioya's wife was supportive of her husband's work only while his focus was on the idea of using one's will to lead a meaningful and successful life, such as the book, *The Laws of Success*. However, once Makoto began talking about curing illness and healing people, she could no longer accept it and she felt he had crossed the line. Like so, I sense that there are various stages of faith in real life.

Also, it seems "academics" was standing in the way of her. Oftentimes, academics could take over people's religious faith. Instead of it creating individuals with qualities like god, it creates many "little gods" based on the level of academic intelligence. So the higher the educational background people attain, the likelier it is for them to lose faith. As a result, they will become self-centered, and have a strong sense of wanting people to 'have faith in them.'

My ex-wife was easily attracted by worldly matters such as "whether a company is a prestigious company or not." As for me, I had more or less surmounted such reputations.

In a conversation between the doctor and Makoto Mioya, there is a scene in which the following line appears: "It seems like the power of faith won in a battle between the leading medical technologies and a new religion." This was what my former wife said to me at the time.

Since the hospital in which I was hospitalized offered advanced medical services and had many outstanding doctors, my wife at the time told me, "Looks like this is a battle between advanced medicine and a new religion." I didn't think she would say that. She looked convinced that modern medicine would win.

Strangely enough, she may have had a very polarized understanding of faith; she defined her faith for medicine and religion as two separate things. This caused our family to face some internal challenges, but as a result, I was also able to start various new activities, such as the missionary tours in Japan and around the world, healing illnesses and starting a political party.

My aim in the beginning was to become Buddha even if I could not share my enlightenment with other people, but many people started to join me along the way. And my illness in 2004 became the turning point for me to start taking action as a Savior. There is a scene in this movie where it very briefly illustrates these moments.

This is the important meaning of my New Resurrection.

Q2 Transitioning of the Mission of Life

Questioner B

In the lecture, you mentioned that the lyrics of the theme song of *Immortal Hero* titled, "New Resurrection" is of the thoughts you had during the lonesome night you spent on your first day at the hospital.

Prior to this, you had already lectured 900 times, and published over 300 books, so you easily could've felt like you had done enough and the end may be close. From such a low point in your life, how did you bring yourself to attaining the New Resurrection? And how did you come to become aware that you were to shift yourself from your mission as a Buddha to start taking action as a Savior? I would be grateful if you could explain to us a little more deeply about how you came to become aware of your mission that kept growing.

I am still known as the "Legendary businessman"

When we are hospitalized all of a sudden and bound to a bed, our minds will wander and think about many things.

When I thought back on myself, I believe I studied very hard in my school days, and as a businessman, I was told that I worked 10 times more than an average person. To this day, I am still known as the "legendary businessman" in a trading house and a rumor of me is still going around.

Just the other day, when my second daughter visited her friend at her company, this story of me came up. The friend was from the first graduating class of Happy Science University (HSU), and is working for a company—that is not run by our believer based on Happy Science principles. The company was a clothing company, but the CEO had hired an HSU graduate because he was a fan of mine.

The CEO had asked the friend if it was possible to meet with my daughter, so my daughter did. She did not quite understand it then, but apparently he told her that he knew me back when I worked in New York City, and also my "code name" too. He was supposedly working at a trust bank at the time and wanted to tell her that he knew about Ryuho Okawa during his New York years. It confused my daughter, but this was what she heard.

He then gave to her neckties and other souvenirs and she happily came home. She then said to me, "I'm not really sure, but the CEO I met today knew about you. He has hired an HSU student, and even gave us gifts."

But when I did a bit of research, I realized there was no way we would have overlapped in New York because of our age difference. Based on the CEO's profile, he had graduated from Keio University in 1994, and I was in New York between 1982 and 1983. So there is at least a 10-year gap, and there is no way we would have met.

So supposedly he started working for the bank in 1994 and left for New York around then. What it means is that this CEO who had gone to New York 10 years after I left had learned and heard stories about me when he got there. But seeing how enthusiastically he spoke as if we had worked together shows that he was a big fan of mine. This certainly shows that I was a "legendary businessman." In this way, I had already worked enough back then, but in addition to that, I established a religion.

Recently, I have been seeing old school friends in my dreams, so perhaps they are thinking of me. There are only a few people who have accomplished so much since World War II, so perhaps they are curious about how far I will go.

What the University of Tokyo graduate doctor told me, And how I responded

You will find a doctor named Dr. Momoyama in the movie, *Immortal Hero*, but I recall a conversation I had with the actual doctor who was the inspiration for Dr. Momoyama.

I believe the publication of *The Laws of Success* was around my 300th book at the time, but this is what I told him: "I have lectured 900 times, and published 300 books, so I feel I have taught enough. The only lectures I haven't been able to give were "The Laws of Twilight Years" or "The Laws of the Elderly." I feel quite regretful, but there is still hope, so I feel I have already done enough in life."

Then, the doctor responded and said, "You are still so young, so you can't have finished just yet." He was an excellent doctor who had graduated from the University of Tokyo and studied abroad at Harvard University. He seemed to have sensed that I was different from a normal, common person from the start. Whenever other doctors would try to take a more materialistic medical approach to treat me, he would do everything he could to stop that from happening.

I actually felt like I had already worked enough in this life and was ready to accept my fate. To tell the truth, when I married my former wife, I asked her if she was still willing to marry me even if I may only live until 48. She replied, "That's 18 years… If we have 18 years of being together then I don't mind." And so we got married. Then I fell ill and was told I may die in May 2004 just before I turned 48 in July of the same year, so what I said was accurate.

That is why I felt like I had accomplished the least I could in my mission at this point. It was very unusual to have been able to publish 300 books, so I think it was truly an achievement.

Starting up three generations worth of work in my time

In this world, there are people who are born into noble families who have had a springboard to jump high from the start. In my case, I was born to an ordinary family from the countryside.

Recently, I watched a Japanese movie called *Tonde Saitama*, which pokes fun at the people of Saitama Prefecture. It was trying to point out how rural Saitama was compared to the 23 wards in Tokyo. If a prefecture with a population of 8 million people is rural, then the prefectures of my hometown Shikoku must seem like an isolated island floating in the southern sea to them.

I thought that the establishment elites of Tokyo may not want to hear another story of someone from the countryside succeeding in Tokyo after much hard work, but I certainly felt like I achieved a good amount as a founder of a religious organization.

Normally, it is not possible for a founder of a religion to construct a building during their time. They might be able to build an office, but their main focus is to compile the doctrine, so even if they give lectures, they usually do not manage to build branches. Branches would usually start getting built by the second generation leader and all other activities, like starting political or educational activities will start after the third generation. The teachings would usually start to spread overseas during the third generation also. This will only happen if the religion succeeds, but even then, it takes three generations to accomplish this much.

In my case, I decided to "set my foot in" all these activities during my time. I could have left the later generation to do the work, but I wanted to accomplish as much as possible and leave behind the general frameworks while I lived. That way, the coming generations would then be able to complete and develop the activities further, so I "set my foot in" deeper.

If a guiding spirit like Jesus or whoever had told me that I still have the mission to give over 2,000 lectures and publish about 2,200 books when I became ill at 47 years of age, I would have considered it as some kind of harsh training. I may have considered the pressure as if I was tied up and been subjected to waterboarding or fire torture. This is how I would have felt back then.

While I was seriously ill, I even wrote nine years' worth of the opening messages (A Guide for the Mind) to the Happy Science monthly magazine, but since I was told that I might die if I kept writing, I stopped there. At the time, I never thought I would be able to accomplish as much work as I have. I had been giving lectures about training oneself, so I just decided to practice it myself through this experience.

The weight of carrying a religious organization In addition to the weight of family

While I couldn't protect my family completely, I tried as much as I could. I just knew that I could not neglect my work in order to protect my family. As the religious organization developed, I also felt that the balance between the public and private affairs of my life changing, and I also found it very difficult to look at myself objectively.

For example, Mr. Carlos Ghosn of Nissan was investigated for criminal charges for mixing his public and private matters (at the time of the lecture). This shows how difficult it is to balance both public and personal affairs even for an executive that is of a world class.

In other words, to my family, I looked strange. The harder and harder I tried to make the organization bigger, and the more results I accumulated, the smaller and smaller I felt inside my family.

Even as the founder and CEO of Happy Science, I started acting timidly and cautiously like a salaried worker and became very cautious about my interactions with my surroundings. To my family, it looked strange. The more progress I made, the more freedom I should have had. But I began to "shrink" as if I was a hired employee.

This is the same in Japan and across the world, and I think this will only be experienced by people who have managed to expand their business to a certain level. This is what I experienced.

Usually, people with leadership skills enjoy developing themselves and self-realizing themselves, and telling people about their experience. For example, even someone like Mr. Shoichi Watanabe, who was known as an opinion leader, didn't have any other responsibility apart from providing for his family. I am sure he had to refute and face many critiques to his own argument, but if he had to carry an entire religious institution on his shoulders in addition to a family like I do, there would be huge amount of pressure.

Basically, I felt a certain responsibility to develop and grow more as a leader. Thinking back, if someone asked me before I was in my 30s about whether I could build such a big religious organization 15 years later, even for someone who was known as a "legendary businessman," I could not be so confident about that.

In the 90s, I was told that every adult in Japan knew me. I became sick after this, so I had to develop myself further and grow our organization (Happy Science) more as a public organization. I knew that I had to carry the weight but the pressure was intense. In this sense, I thought it was a kind of challenge to see if I was spiritually strong to endure and overcome the illness.

For example, say you just had a heart attack, get taken to a hospital, and are told that you need immediate surgery, and that an organ transplant is the only way for you to live. At this stage, do you think you can think about building a big organization later? Could you think about building local branches and temples all over, go on missionary tours in Japan and around the world, create movies, establish a political party, and start a university? I'm sure it's difficult to think of doing all of this after you are told that you need an organ transplant and have to wait for the right organ donor. Normally, all people can think about is if they can return home to their family or not.

I had no fear of death since I am an expert of the afterlife

Even so, this is not so simple. I not only knew about life and death, I was already a kind of expert of the world after death. In other words, I had already been interacting with spirits from the world after death for over 20 years as part of my job and publishing their messages. They had been helping me during my lectures also. I was actually already having communications with people in the afterlife and I am sure that there isn't anyone else who knew about both life and death any more than I did. So in truth, I had no fear in terms of life and death that any normal person might have.

Usually, people think that death is the ultimate end and may feel like that is end of the world. To me, death is not a distant world but more like a world right outside my window. As soon as I open the window, it would take me straight into the afterlife. This is the kind of life I've been living, so it would be embarrassing if I feared death.

Usually it is said that the most pitiful sight to see is when someone like a high Buddhist monk is in a hospital bed with terminal cancer. They would apparently say, "I don't want to die, I don't want to die."

When they are told that they only have, for example, half a year, three months or one month to live, they would say, "I don't want to die. I don't know what will happen to me when I die." They can't help but feel anxious. I've heard that this is most shameful to see.

Unlike these high priests who only do spiritual training in this world without any knowledge of the afterlife, I knew about the other world, so in that sense I had no fear.

I have lived like there is no tomorrow

What the guiding spirits, like Edgar Cayce and Jesus, who were visiting me at the time were telling me is, "You will recover, so you must resurrect!" At the time, I did not have the mind to plan the next several decades of my work, but I made efforts to progress one step or even two steps more by simply improving every day of my life as I worked to build strength. I truly felt like I was on an army crawl. I was ready to move forward even if it meant that I had to drag myself.

"I'm ready to die any time. It could be one year later, three years later, or even five years later." I told myself this, and each and every day, I was ready to reset my life. Like so, I was living so that I was ready to die at any point.

Even during my rehabilitation, I said to myself, "If I am going to die, I should have no attachments. I may feel attached to this world if I have Japanese and world classic books I had not read, so why don't I finish reading all of them now while I am loosely supervised. It shouldn't matter if I finish reading the books before I fully recover." So I read a large number of classics from Japan and around the world. In this meaning, I feel I was given some resting time.

So at this point, I cannot say confidently that I was able to see my future. And the discussions about my health from a worldly perspective made me anxious. Either way, I told myself "I'll live by the motto, 'Today is my whole life'," and of course "Die for the Truth." I believed that I was given another life and wanted to do as much as I could. This may have been close to suicidal tendencies or this willingness to die could have been what kept me alive, but the more I pushed myself with the willingness to die, the stronger my body became. This is strange indeed. I was surprised how far I kept going.

What to abandon, what to choose

I cannot explain this enough, but during my lonesome night, I was thinking about the whole city, the whole world, and various other things. My mind wandered and thought about the lifestyles of various families, the politics in Japan, the mass media, education, and also the people living all around the world, people in countries where there are risks of wars, and so on.

And then I realized that there was still a tremendous amount of work left even if I may have done enough to self-realize. I also thought, "If I truly believe that I am El Cantare, then I need to accomplish more than what Buddha and Jesus did." I knew I had not reached there yet, so I felt I needed to level up my work. I still feel the same today. In a way, I feel like I have lived a few lives already, and since I am rarely born into this world, I wanted to live to the fullest when I am born and live eagerly.

Life in the end is about what you choose. You have to choose one from many things, so you will have to abandon something to gain another thing. Each time, you would ask yourself, "What should I abandon and what should I choose." If your boat were to sink, you would throw out all your valuable items. So the question is, "What is the last thing you will keep?" In this way, the teachings of 'Today is my whole life' and 'Die for the Truth' are very important.

Normally, if a husband decides to live with the spirit of Dying for the Truth, he may be treated like he has gone insane by his family. He will probably be told, "There is no way you have such a mission," and that may be the end. So sometimes it is important to decide on your mission by yourself.

And now, 15 years have passed since my illness, I still have so much motivation that even my sons are starting to get annoyed. I am starting to think that I should hide my enthusiasm a little bit more.

So even if I say that I may not live much longer, I will persevere. I am a little worried that some may say it is really troublesome for me to be so ambitious. But since I can rarely come to this world, I would be grateful if you would allow me to work for another five, ten extra years.

I am hoping to see my potential as a religious leader and see how much I can do and how far I can go.

AFTERWORD

I published *The New Resurrection* under the same title of the book written by the main character of the movie, Makoto Mioya (his name was taken from Ameno-Mioya-Gami* [literally: the great Father God of the universe]). I have lived each day thinking, "Today is my whole life," and I also nearly died at 47, but it seems I am now 63. At this age, Nichiren and Kukai had already finished their mission and returned to Heaven.

Shakyamuni Buddha continued to give his teachings until he was 80 years of age (equivalent to 120 years nowadays). My next goal for now would be like this.

If it is allowed, I wish to continue working until I'm over 90 like Shinran.

Even a part of my soul is born into this world only once in 3,000 years. The core consciousness of El Cantare will not be reborn again at least for the next 150 million years. I wish to continue preaching these laws so they reach as many people as possible.

Ryuho Okawa
Founder and CEO of Happy Science Group
Aug. 15, 2019

---

* TF: Ameno-Mioya-Gami is the creator god who appears in an ancient Japanese text called "Hotsuma Tsutae," a document that is said to be older than the Japanese mythic texts, "Kojiki" and "Nihon Shoki."

Translator's note: In May, 2004, the author wrote 108 opening messages while he was hospitalized. Of the 108 messages, 15 messages, that are associated to Chapter One and Two of this book, were carefully selected and inserted.

Chapter Three

A GUIDE FOR THE MIND

-Special Selection-

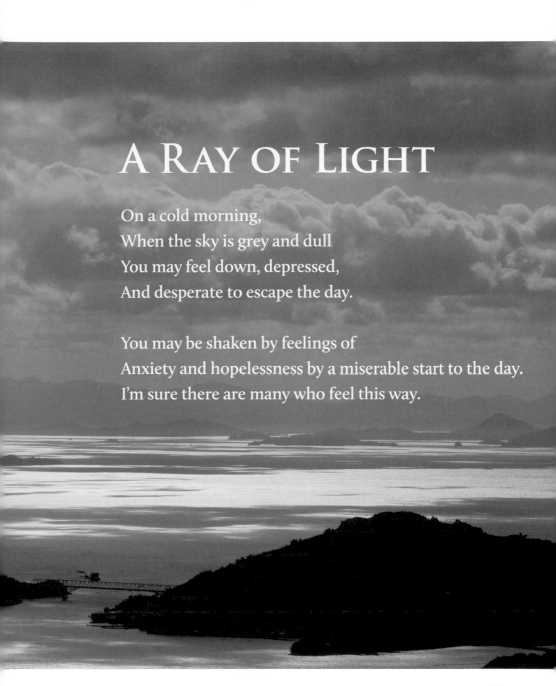

A Ray of Light

On a cold morning,
When the sky is grey and dull
You may feel down, depressed,
And desperate to escape the day.

You may be shaken by feelings of
Anxiety and hopelessness by a miserable start to the day.
I'm sure there are many who feel this way.

But
The moment a ray of bright light
Breaks through the clouds from the sky
And shines in,
The world changes dramatically.
Everything changes dramatically.
Trees shine in brilliant green,
And flowers would smile and begin to greet.

This is the power of faith.
This is the great mercy of God.
Shine a ray of light in your heart also.
You, yourself, must become a ray of light.

When You Truly Love Someone…

Some people finally realize
That they loved their partner
After they've separated in an argument.

There are husbands who, after having divorced,
Feel surprised at how empty life is without their wives.

There are wives who,
After greatly abusing their husbands and finding some peace,
Realize the greatness of their husbands.
There are parents who, after they've lost their child,
Continue to blame themselves for not praising their child.

Now, everyone, listen carefully.
Once they're gone, it's too late.
If you love someone,
Tell them that you love them
Right now.
If you like someone,
Show them that you like them
Right now.

Don't let it become an eternal regret.
While alive,
When you love someone,
When you truly love someone,
Tell them.
Tell them completely.

THE POWER OF VISUALIZATION

Visualize
That you've bounced back.

Visualize
Yourself energetic,
Healthy,
And full of energy.

Visualize
Your family happy
And your home as the foundation of utopia.

Visualize
You and your spouse overcoming difficulties
Living together for the rest of your days
For the bond between a couple spans
Past, present, and future.

Visualize
The light of faith going into your whole body
Curing any serious illness you might have.

Visualize yourself
Blessed with supporters,
Blessed with money,
And succeeding in your work.

Visualize
Your children
Growing into wonderful adults.

Visualizing
Is what determines your future.
Thoughts that you repeatedly dispatch
Will surely be realized.

MODERN MEDICINE AND RELIGION

How should the relationship between
Modern medicine and religion be understood?
This is a difficult topic. It must be so.

But I believe
Modern medicine is also guided by God.
Suppose the light of angels in the medical field
Are called "gods of medicine,"
And we trace down these gods' roots (origin),
You will always reach God Hermes.

Also, at the roots of Western medicine
And its sometimes opponent, Eastern medicine,
You will discover Taoism and Buddhism.
There are many cases in the past
Of monks' teaching medicine.

Of course, gods are also actively cooperating
With religions that help people to cure their illness.
Time to time, they make miracles happen
To enhance people's faith.

What's important is for medicine and religion
To harmonize and cooperate with each other.
Doctors who appreciate faith
Use the power of their mind to cure more illnesses.
By using both words and medicine together,
Serious illness may even be miraculously cured.

And if religious leaders
Cooperate with where there is light in medicine,
The amount of distressed people
That could be saved will be greater.
They both aim to make people happy,
So ideally, they should help each other.

LET US LEARN TO FORGIVE EACH OTHER

To hate someone is easy.
But to forgive someone is difficult.

People do not want to think
That their unhappiness is their own fault.
It's painful to admit that you're hurt
Because of your foolishness.
You would always want to blame someone else.
You would want to blame it on your company,
Your country or the era.

I guess other people may be foolish too
Just like yourself.
There will be people who are too cruel to accept.
There will be people who you cannot get along with.

I also get hurt and suffer
In my modest fight
Surrounded by atheists and materialists.

I feel upset at just how small the amount of love I have is.
I'm ashamed of my lack of tolerance.
I shed tears from my lack of wisdom.
I suffer because the people suffer—this is how I feel.

All people are equal before death.
Remember that one day, it will be your last day.
So let us learn to forgive each other.

LIFE IS A WORKBOOK OF PROBLEMS

"Life is a workbook of problems."
This phrase is very wise indeed.
The more years I train in this life,
The deeper I find these words to be.

Everything in your life is caused by
The seeds that you sow in your mind
And also in the way that you nurture those seeds.
It also depends on
How you interact with other people
As well as how you think and act about
The relationship between you
And the world that surrounds you.

If you understand the laws of cause and effect
You should know that
You can solve your own problems in life
By dint of your own efforts.

What do you think is righteous
And what is evil to you?

What actions do you think
Are in accordance with God,
And what action do you think
Are doings of evils?
It all depends on the choices and decisions
That you make every day.
The collection of these answers
Will be the sum total of your life

You must humbly be ready to accept that
The judgment you will receive in the afterlife
Will be based not on your fate, but on the efforts you made.

THE LIGHT THAT SHINES UPON THE WORLD

Your future will be dark
If you think that your future is dark.
Your future will be bright
If you think that your future is bright.
Your thoughts are actually
Attracting various happenings and phenomena
That will occur in your future.

Our minds are like magnets
The thought which you always dispatch
Will decide where and in which direction you will go.

So you must be careful of people
Who always say negative things.
When such kinds of people fail at something
Or something bad happens to them,
They will escape responsibility by saying,
"See, it's exactly what I said."
They'll feel like they've protected themselves
And feel proud.
This is a kind of egotism.
People who are intelligent, but are not competent at work,
Are often like this.

If you feel you are taken over by negativity,
Read positive words,
Smile,
And repeatedly say,
"Every day is amazing.
Every day is a new start.
Every day is full of hope."
You, yourself, can become
The light that shines upon the world.

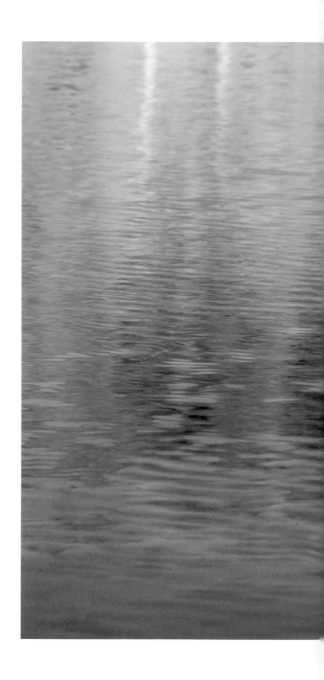

SEPARATION AT DEATH

Death is very saddening.
It is also painful.
Living beings want to continue living
For as long as they have life.
Humans too.
They will continue to live
Until one day, they fall ill or grow old
And be taken away by a messenger of death.

Death separates married couples,
And makes parents and children unable to see each other.
You know in your head
The teachings of the pain of parting from the people you love.
Yet, tears will fall endlessly like a stream.
Even Buddha's words that say
The love for your family is essentially attachment
Will sound very cold-hearted.

When life ends in this world
And you have to separate from your loved ones
It hurts, it's painful, and it's sad.
I know.
It is.
But remember, people are equal in the name of death.
Find solace in knowing
That you can see them again in the afterlife.

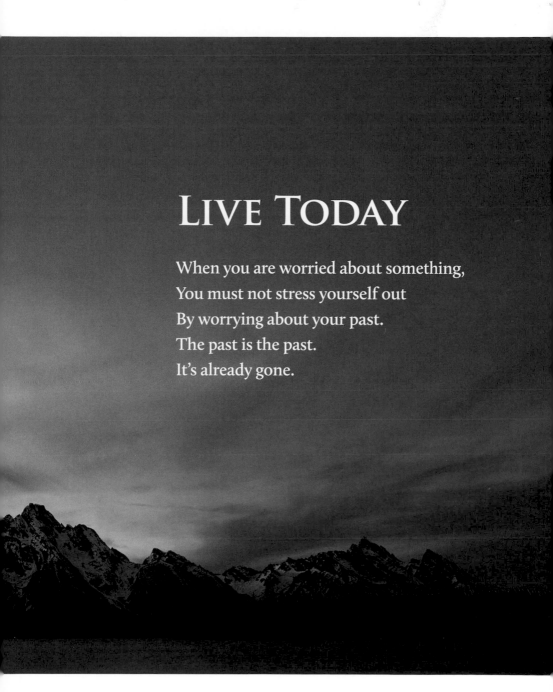

LIVE TODAY

When you are worried about something,
You must not stress yourself out
By worrying about your past.
The past is the past.
It's already gone.

You must not use today's energy
By stressing over your past.
This is important.
Why worry about past mistakes or wrong decisions?
Why does it matter
That you've been criticized by other people?

You are alive today.
You cannot use yesterday's time.
You cannot use tomorrow's time.

The only time you actually have
Is the 24 hours you have today.
All you need is food for today.
All you need is work for today.

So just live today.
Don't worry about the future.
Leave tomorrow's work for tomorrow.
Live today the best you can.

Your Mind and Health

70 to 80 percent of illnesses are caused by
Conflicts and stressful thinking in your mind.
The other 20 to 30 percent is caused by
Physical influences.

When we look into your worries
We will know what illness you might have
In the future.
When we know what illness you have
We will know why you are worried.

If you have fears or worries in your mind,
It will manifest on your body as illness.
That is because your mind and body are connected.
So by healing your mind,
Your health will recover.

This is the basic truth.
There are millions of harmful substances to a human body.

Such as viruses that are everywhere on Earth.
Yet, some become ill
And some don't.

Check yourself in the light of Buddha's Truth
And find where you have strayed from the Middle Way.
By doing so,
You can protect yourself from and also cure your illness.

YOUR MIND
AND ILLNESS

Cancer is caused by
Work that is beyond your capability, overwork,
Unresolved human relationship problems,
Overeating and overdrinking due to stress,
And thoughts of grudge and hatred.

Heart disease, stomach ulcers,
And diabetes are caused by
Lingering worries,
Anxiety or an overly stressful lifestyle.
In other words,
They are the cost of living in a competitive society
As well as anger and self-destructive thoughts.
High-calorie foods, excessive fluid intake,
And lack of exercise
Supports its outbreak even more.

Illness of blood vessels and the brain
Occurs if you are overly worried about the past or the future,
Or you're constantly speaking ill and complaining
About things in your life.
In other words,
People who are suffering from their unsatisfied pride
Would develop these illnesses.
Their mind's "excretory functions" are weak.

Skin problems develop
When the blood is dirty from
Excessive eating and drinking
Caused by the fear and stress that you have
In your personal relationship.

Illness of the joints
Is often caused by spiritual possession
That comes from some conflict in the mind or resentment.

Faith, rest, an unattached mind,
A smile, a positive mind, and looking after your health,
Should cure it all.

THE ROAD TO BE IMPERISHABLE

Life in this world is transient.
A hundred years at most
Of dreaming in this illusion.

As you live the remaining years you have left in this life,
You must keep in mind that you will one day
Return to the Real World, the world of eternal life.

Many things will be left undone.
You will have a mountain of attachments to this life.
It will be painful to leave behind your loved ones.
Your company, your work, your fortune—
I'm sure there'll be many reasons to be worried.

But listen.
There is an unwavering principle
That separates this world and the other world.
Your mind is all you can take back with you.

So steadily prepare yourself for that day,
And continue making efforts diligently.
The road to be imperishable
Is to live together with the Truth.
Let us walk this road together.
Now,
Go straightly on and on with courage and perseverance.

Oh
How Blessed
We Are

Oh how blessed we are.
We can see with both eyes.
We can hear sounds with both ears.
We can carry things with both arms.
And we can walk with both legs.
I'm sure no one will want to give any of these away
Even if they are given millions of dollars.

Oh how blessed we are.
We can breathe through our lungs without thinking,
And our heart continues beating without a minute of rest
And our stomach and intestines digest the food we eat.
It is so wonderful that
We have a brain to think
And even memorize things with.
Words let us tell others' our thoughts too.
It's like magic.

Oh how blessed we are.
We can read books,
Enjoy music,
Watch TV,
And what's more, we even have a family.

It's wonderful to be able to live.
It's wonderful that we have today and to have tomorrow.
Life is so sweet and beautiful.

A Brief Journey

The day will equally come to anyone.
We are equal before death ——
The fear of death,
The pain and the sadness will always be there
Even if your lifespan were to increase to 200 or 300 years.

Religion will continue to exist
Even in future societies.
No matter how beautiful this world may look,
No matter how much medicine may develop,
Without religion
People will not be able to overcome the fear of death.
And then
Those who are the first to overcome the fear of death
Will become heroes and awakened ones.

When you are halfway through your life
Slowly,
Start removing your attachments to this world.

Be less eager for fame,
And purify your selfish desires and make it clearer.
Even if you have wealth,
You cannot take it back with you.
Value a mind that is less angry
And calm.

From the perspective of the other world,
Life in this world is just a brief journey.

SEEK FOR
THE WAY IN LIFE

This world on earth,
This materialistic world,
There is a whirlpool of desires in this world.
Status, fame,
Power, money,
Conflict over love affairs,
The convenience of materialistic things,
There are endless desires that grow in the mind
Of wanting this and that.

We all need some desire and ambition
To live in this world.
But what you must always remember are
Peace of mind,
And the completion of "the way."

The phrase "peace of mind"
May sound passive to some people.
But to have peace of mind, you need
Strong will, courage, and diligent efforts.
Too many people are still unaware
Of the true power of a calm mind.

Triumph over selfish desires,
The desire to self-preserve, and egotism,
And always seek the way to your inner self,
And make the completion of the way your lifelong goal.

Do not forget a guide for the mind.

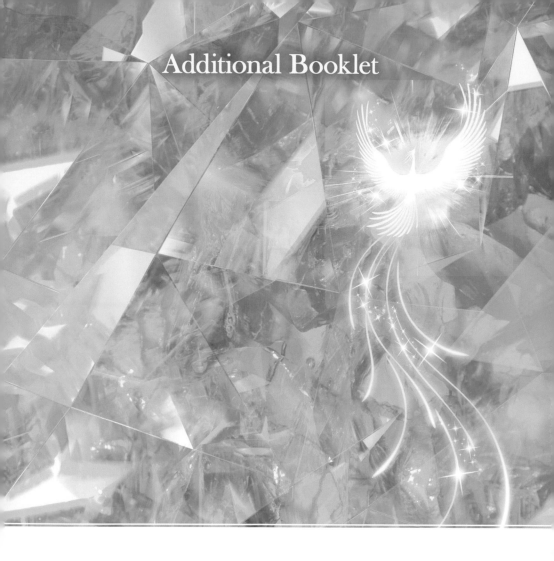

Additional Booklet

Today is My Whole Life
&
Die for the Truth

Records of Ryuho Okawa

Happy Science International Headquarters
Happy Science General Headquarters

With the Savior, live through

Deciding what is light and what is darkness,

Or what is good and what is evil in the same age –

This is the power of a Savior.

It is also the wish of a Savior.

Indicating the true direction

That people should move forward,

Leading them to stop doing evil and choose goodness,

Opening the way to the next life –

This is the mission of a Savior.

In politics,

It would be to create a barrier

To prevent hell from forming on earth.

This is also important.

your life for others and the world

Please purify your mind and make it clear.

Always return to the starting point and tell yourself,

"Throughout the hundred-year life given to me,

I shall live for others and the world."

This is important.

And, in order to keep this attitude,

It is essential you live as you always stay awakened

To spirituality.

From the lecture, "A Savior's Wish" given on April 29, 2019

Born on July 7, 1956, the Great Enlightenment at 24, and his time in Tokyo and New York

"I remember that I loved the way it felt to make an effort to achieve something of higher dimensions, something sublime."

From El Cantare in His Youth

Master Ryuho Okawa was born in Kawashima-cho (now the city of Yoshinogawa), Oe District, Tokushima Prefecture at seven o'clock in the morning on July 7, 1956. He worked hard at his studies from early childhood and went on to enter the University of Tokyo, Faculty of Law. He studied day and night, motivated by his aspiration to integrate various academic subjects. Just after two o'clock in the afternoon on March 23, 1981, days before his graduation from university, he experienced automatic writing. The words, "Good News, Good News" which mean "Gospel" in the Christian context, were written. This was the moment of the Great Awakening.

The managing director of a major trading company, an alumni of the University of Tokyo, personally recruited him to join the company that spring. Spiritual communications with the heavenly world continued while he was working at the trading company's head office in Tokyo. Shakyamuni Buddha, Master Okawa's branch spirit, appeared to him in July and proclaimed that Master Okawa is the spiritual being named El Cantare, and that it is his mission to save all living creatures by spreading Buddha's teachings.

Yoshino River runs through Tokushima Prefecture, the birthplace of Master Okawa.

(L) The annex Master Okawa used for studying since fourth grade. He used the southern room upstairs to study. The building has been demolished.

He was a member of the kendo club in high school. (R) He engaged diligently in his studies and club activities, even studying during lunchtime. (L) His kendo attire while at university.

"In the soft spring sunlight on the afternoon of March 23, 1981, (...) I suddenly sensed the presence of an invisible being in my room. (...) Then, my hand holding the pencil began to move on its own volition and wrote, iishirase, iishirase (Good News, Good News) on many cards."

From The Laws of the Sun

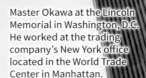

Master Okawa at the Lincoln Memorial in Washington, D.C. He worked at the trading company's New York office located in the World Trade Center in Manhattan.

Resignation at 30, renunciation, founding of Happy Science, and its miraculous expansion to the world

In 1986, at the age of 30, Master Okawa resigned from the trading company and founded Happy Science in October of that year. He gave his first lecture titled, "For the Launching of Happy Science," on November 23 (the event is called The First Turning of the Wheel of Truth). An audience of 87 attended from all over Japan.

"For the next 50 years or so,
I will hold lectures for you and produce writings.
I think that I can achieve great things in 50 years."

From the lecture "For the Launching of Happy Science"

Master Okawa giving his first lecture on Nov. 23, 1986. The First Turning of the Wheel of Truth lasted for 2.5 hours, including the Q&A session.

His first public lecture, "The Principles of Happiness," which was held four months later, attracted an audience five times as many. The audience continued to increase at subsequent lectures and seminar courses held by Master Okawa. A series of lectures held at huge venues such as Makuhari Messe in 1990 were packed, and in 1991, there was a massive 50,000 audience for a special grand lecture at Tokyo Dome.

In his second public lecture, "The Principle of Love," which was given in the early days of Happy Science, Master Okawa announced his future vision of Happy Science for the next 30 years. He spoke of reforming fields such as politics, education, culture and the arts, and of expanding overseas, and those prophecies are now coming true.

The vision for the next 30 years predicted in the lecture "The Principle of Love" (1987)

STAGE 1

The winds of religious reformation will blow throughout Japan in the next decade.

STAGE 2

The fundamental reformation in flelds such as politics, education, culture and the arts, and reforms in corporate systems.

STAGE 3

20 or 30 years from now, our publications will be available worldwide, and the campaign for Utopia will ripple out from Japan and spread around the world.

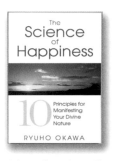

See *The Science of Happiness*, Chapter 2 [New York: Destiny Books, 2009]

(L) Taken on October 6, 1986 at the office in Suginami Ward, Tokyo, where Happy Science was founded. This 10 m^2 room was the starting point.

(R) The site of the First Turning of the Wheel of Truth, Nippori Shuhan Kaikan. It's now known as Happy Science Commemoration Hall of the First Turning of the Wheel of Truth.

In 1990, many bookshops across Japan set up special sections specifically for Master's books.

Taken on March 18, 1995. Believers voluntarily held a protest in Tokyo calling for an official investigation of Aum Shinrikyo. The police were encouraged by this, and conducted a search of Aum Shinrikyo facilities four days later.

Later, the police sent a letter of gratitude to Happy Science.

In October 1990, IRH Press began setting up booths at book fairs all over the world. Taken in Frankfurt, Germany.

"We used Tokyo Dome for five years or so from 1991, but in the end, even Tokyo Dome wasn't big enough. We even joked about floating a tanker in the Pacific Ocean as a venue. Anyway, things just snowballed like that."

From the lecture, "The Spirit of a Religious Nation"

Tokyo Dome

The first-ever Celebration of the Lord's Descent was advertised in the front page of Japanese newspapers

The Sankei Newspaper June 13, 1991 issue

(C) The December 7, 1991 issue of *Financial Times*. It featured an exclusive interview with Master Okawa, who stated the arrival of a golden age for Japan.

(B) Taken on July 10, 1992 in Tokyo Dome, at the Celebration of the Lord's Descent. The lecture title was, "Initiation." Tens of thousands gathered at the venue.

To save each and every human soul, building the infrastructure of happiness throughout the world

"I am building shojas and local temples of Happy Science
as lighthouses to light up the dark seas.
I would like these lighthouses
to give out a bright and powerful light."

From On the Mission

Tokyo Shoshinkan opened on December 8, 2001. It was the first main temple built in the center of a city.

In 1996, 10 years after the founding, Happy Science built its first large-scale main temple, Head Temple Shoshinkan (in Utsunomiya, Tochigi Prefecture). Many large-scale main temples have been built all over Japan since then. Furthermore, Happy Science began putting energy into constructing its local temples in April 2002.

• Main Temples in Japan •

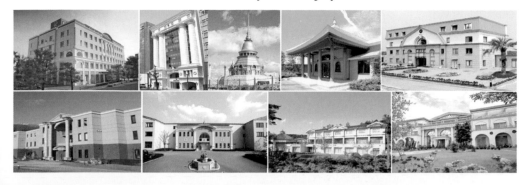

Over 700 Large-scale main temples, local temples, branches, and missionary centers in the world

as of November 2019

About 10,000 Missionary houses

For more information, http://happy-science.org

• Local Temples in Japan •

Hokushinetsu 31
Kinki 67
Chugoku 33
Kyushu 62

Hokkaido 20
Tohoku 26
Kanto 70
Tokyo 36
Tokai 40
Shikoku 23

Each of these facilities has its own role. The large-scale main temples are venues for genuine religious training, and the local temples function as lighthouses that light up their local communities and as venues for salvation work.

*"I wish to build as many as I can,
and I wish for them to shine more brightly,
to an infinite height with infinite strength."*

From On the Mission

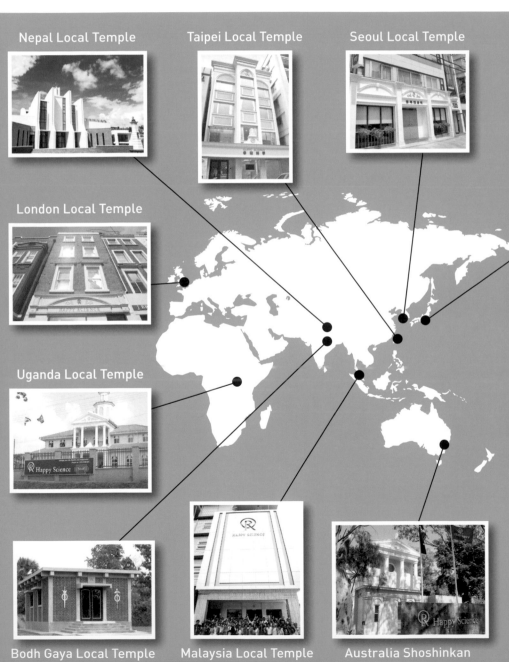

Nepal Local Temple

Taipei Local Temple

Seoul Local Temple

London Local Temple

Uganda Local Temple

Bodh Gaya Local Temple

Malaysia Local Temple

Australia Shoshinkan

• Temples Worldwide •

Our movement has spread overseas as well. In December 2006, we built Hawaii Shoja, our first main temple overseas. Since then, we have also built one in Brazil and in Australia. In addition, we have also begun constructing local temples. We are setting up a network of light around the world.

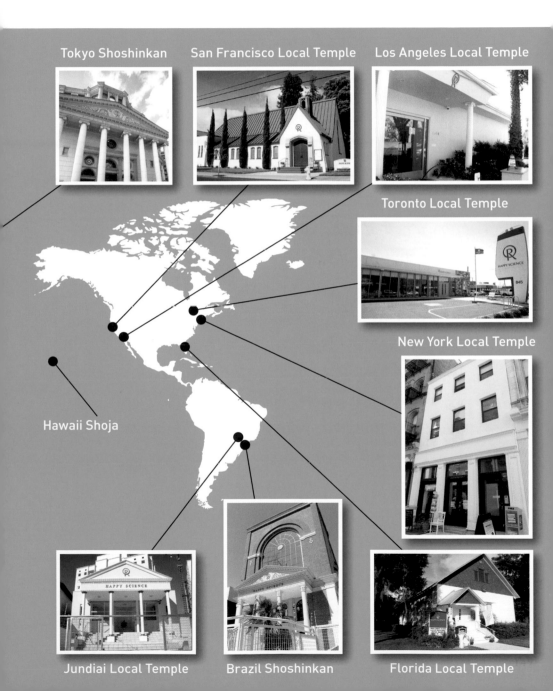

Tokyo Shoshinkan

San Francisco Local Temple

Los Angeles Local Temple

Toronto Local Temple

New York Local Temple

Hawaii Shoja

Jundiai Local Temple

Brazil Shoshinkan

Florida Local Temple

I became Buddha at the age of 24,
Started teaching at 30,
And had my third death at the age of 47,
In the physical meaning.
I, myself, is a resurrection.
I am a rebirth.
I made up my mind to become a Savior
from a Buddha last year.
This is the meaning of my third death. I think so.
I was a Buddha.
I'm now a real Buddha but I need to be a Savior.
It's the meaning of my third death.
This whole world, or universe,
Gave me another life and told me
That I have a remaining mission.
Please spread these lectures all over the world.
This is my desire, my work, and my mission.
I made up my mind last year and said "I lay down my life."
"Lay down my life" means fushaku shimmyo in Japanese.
I made up my mind to lay down my life,
So I made a lot of speeches in every local branch in Japan.
I want to go abroad
And spread these lectures to the end of this life.

You should know that El Cantare is the real Buddha
And its mission includes a Savior's mission.
I, myself, is a resurrection.

From About An Unshakable Mind

About An Unshakable Mind
[Available only at our main
and local temples, and
branches. See end pages for
contact information.]

As mentioned in Chapters 1 and 2 of this book, Master Okawa suffered a severe heart attack on May 14, 2004. The doctor at the hospital ran some tests and informed him, "Your heart is not contracting. Since your heart has stopped, you are dead." He was hospitalized even though he was medically assessed as "dead," and was placed in the intensive care unit.

While there, Master Okawa affirmed his own resurrection and commenced his sacred work. He proofread his book, *The Laws of Success* (published in September 2004) and wrote nine years' worth of opening messages, "A Guide for the Mind," for the Happy Science Monthly Magazine (See Chapter 3). He was discharged from the hospital two weeks later.

These facts were first revealed four years later in his lecture, "About *An Unshakable Mind*." In it, Master Okawa reminisced about that time, speaking about his 'third death' and how he made up his mind to do missionary work as a Savior, prepared to die for the Truth.

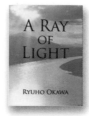

A Ray of Light
[Available only
at our main and
local temples, and
branches. See end
pages.]

A Guide for the Mind is on the introduction page of
the Happy Science Monthly Magazine

Master's miraculous resurrection—to save every soul through his missionary lectures all over the world

"Throughout the year 2007, (...) I also shared with you at every opportunity I had, about the importance of having courage, and taking on challenges."
"I have not only talked about it;
I have also put it into action myself,
making visits to local temples throughout Japan,
and traveling even further distances to our temples overseas."

From My Lover, Cross the Valley of Tears

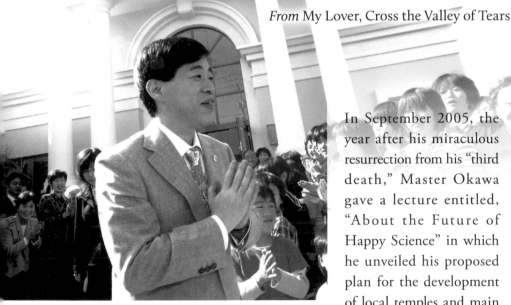

Oct. 28, 2007 Takamatsu Local Temple

In September 2005, the year after his miraculous resurrection from his "third death," Master Okawa gave a lecture entitled, "About the Future of Happy Science" in which he unveiled his proposed plan for the development of local temples and main temples up until 2100.

Two years later, he began a missionary tour* of Japan. It started at the Hiroshima Temple on June 26, and lasted for two years; by December 2009, he had visited all of Japan's 47 prefectures. In addition to that, he also gave his first overseas lecture in English at the Hawaii Branch in 2007. This historic lecture was his First Turning of the Wheel of Truth overseas, and it set the cogs in full motion for his mission as a World Teacher.

*Missionary Tour: Master's visit to local regions to spread the Truth.

Making Humankind Happy: Presenting the Future Vision

On September 25, 2005, in a lecture titled, "About the Future of Happy Science," Master presented the future vision of Happy Science.

Start of the Missionary Tour around Japan

Sep. 19, 2007 Oita Local Temple

Aug. 26, 2007 Sendai-minami Local Temple

Nov. 3, 2007 Musashino Local Temple

Nov. 11, 2007 Kyoto-chuo Local Temple

Oct. 8, 2007 Suginami Local Temple

Start of the Missionary Tour around the world

*"If El Cantare is with you,
There are no enemies."*

From Be Positive

Nov. 18, 2007 Hawaii Branch
First official lecture overseas:
"Be Positive"

153

Lectures are printed as they were spoken; 1,300 books published in 2,190 days

"I truly want these major issues of North and South Korea and of China to be resolved during my time."

From the lecture, "The Power to believe" given on February 11, 2017

For the past few years, Master Ryuho Okawa has published his writings at a pace of roughly one book every 1.7 days. His works are published for the purpose of proving the existence of the Spirit World, of heaven and hell, of the many spiritual beings ranging from gods to spirits of hell, and of resolving various issues that confront people living in this world. In his lectures, Master Okawa speaks clearly and accessibly about current affairs as well as more academic themes, and the lectures are then published in written form. Countless people continue to learn from them.

Since 1985, **2,600 BOOKS** have been published

MIRACULOUS
MILESTONE
3000
RYUHO OKAWA
OVER 3,000 LECTURES!!
AND OVER 2,600 BOOKS

More than 3,000 lectures given to the people

printed as books

Maruzen Marunouchi Bookstore, Tokyo

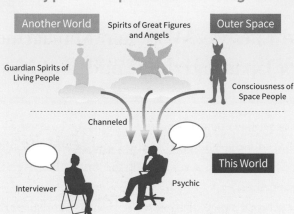

Types of Spiritual Messages

Another World

Guardian Spirits of Living People

Spirits of Great Figures and Angels

Outer Space

Consciousness of Space People

Channeled

Interviewer

Psychic

This World

(A) Taken on April 19, 2018 during "Ryotaro Shiba Speaks On Patriotism," a publicly recorded spiritual message, in the form of an interview.

Lectures: words by Master Okawa's own consciousness

In the lectures, Master Okawa's words are based on his own true thoughts and enlightenment. Compared to 'spiritual messages' where he transmits unaltered words of diverse spirits, the lectures are universal teachings with great power to make people happy. He has also given more than 150 lectures in English (as of Dec. 2019).

Space-people readings

A space-people reading is the act of retrieving the memories of an alien soul who has or had been incarnated on Earth. The person conducting the reading can also summon the alien consciousness of the person concerned and have it speak.

Note:
There are other readings performed in public, such as remote-viewing where Master Okawa spiritually observes a distant location.
Spiritual messages are the opinions of the spirits, so they may sometimes say things that differ from the opinions of the Happy Science Group.

Spiritual messages: words of spiritual beings

Spiritual messages are a spiritual phenomenon where he summons a spirit and narrates that spirit's thoughts and words. The spirit extracts the words it needs from the language center (part of brain that processes and produces speech) of the person conveying the spiritual message, which enables the spirit to speak in its preferred language. More than 1,000 public spiritual messages have been recorded, and more than 500 of such books have been published (as of Dec. 2019).

Spiritual messages from guardian spirits

A guardian spirit is a part of your own soul, in other words, what is also known as your subconscious. Spiritual messages from guardian spirits are a phenomenon where the summoner contacts the subconscious of the person concerned, so the messages are the true thoughts deep in his or her heart.

and translated into 3I LANGUAGES

Eslite Bookstore, Taipei

Kulturkaufhaus Dussmann Bookstore, Berlin

Indigo Bay&Bloor Bookstore, Toronto

In 2011, he won the Guinness World Record for "the most books written in one year by an individual," after publishing 52 books in 2010 alone.

Healthy Mind and Lifestyle, Work and Management, Future Visions of Japan and the World, and More

Master Ryuho Okawa has so far given 3,000 lectures and published 2,600 books. Roughly 70% of them are the teachings of the mind, but overall, they cover many different genres.

The lectures cover a broad range of topics: the mindset and lifestyle that leads to happiness, managing a company, leading a country, resolving international conflicts, etc. They address various doubts that arise in these rapidly changing times and offer timely responses to social issues. We hope you will find a topic that will interest you.

What Happens After Death? What is the Meaning of Life?

- What happens when we die?
- What is the true meaning of life?
- Overcoming the grief of losing a loved one
- A person's past life, the tendency of his soul, his future destiny   ...and more

- Developing a mindset and disposition to keep illness away
- Rejuvenating your mind
- Maintaining your vitality
- Building heartwarming relations
- Developing habits that can rejuvenate your brain and body   ...and more

Youth and Agelessness

Memorial Services

- Dealing with regrets in life
- Try to be forgiving and thankful
- Is my memorial service effective?
- Checkpoints in a memorial service   ..and more

- Coping with cancer, depression, or other illness
- When the doctor tells you, "You won't be cured"
- Dealing with chronic illness
- Healing the illness of your loved one   ...and more

Recovering from Illness

Family Issues

- Worries about your marriage
- Getting along with your in-laws
- Balancing work and family
- Ending the string of bad luck in your family
- Bringing happiness into your family

...and more

- Teaching what is right from wrong
- Teaching the wisdom for success
- Teaching perseverance

...and more

Raising Children Successfully

Developing Good Character, Confidence, and Tolerance

- When counselling helps little
- You can become the real you and be kinder
- Cultivating greater tolerance
- Becoming a dependable leader

...and more

- Interactions at work
- Finding your vocation
- Seeking praise and popularity
- Learning the basics of management
- Changing careers
- Complaints about promotion

...and more

Promotion, Vocation, and Work and Management Abilities

Foresight On the Future of International Politics

- How will the Trump Revolution, the North Korean and Chinese threat, terrorism, and conflicts influence your work and family, and your company's performance and overseas expansion?

...and more

- Future information on politics and economy not reported by the mass media, improving your net income, improving your company's business and finding a successor, planning your post-retirement, how your country can defend itself, and how its politics can be improved

...and more

Reality of Politics and Economy Not Reported by the Media

The Truth of the Universe

- Space people have been coming to Earth
- Space people come in UFOs
- Why do space people come to Earth?
- The future of Earth

...and more

All sorts of miracles will occur when the Savior unleashes His power

"From now on, I believe there will be ten or a hundred times more cases of illnesses healing. (...) With stronger faith, we should gradually see more miracles."

From the book,
The Way to Definite Health

On January 1, 2007, three years after the miraculous resurrection from his 'third death', Master Okawa published *The Laws of Resurrection*. Then, in a seminar based on that book (held on January 27, 2007), he gave the lecture, "The Resurrection of Wellness." In it he said, "The ability of regeneration dwells in the human body. As your faith grows stronger, many kinds of amazing miracles occur." And just as he said, our believers have since been experiencing miracles, one after another.

During Master Okawa's nationwide tour of Happy Science branches in Japan since June 2007, a whole string of miraculous recoveries occurred in the places he visited. In addition, a steady stream of miracles started to occur as a result of ritual prayers such as "Prayer to Eradicate Cancer Cells" performed at branches and temples.

My scoliosis of 40 years was fully cured!

I had been suffering from a curved spine since childhood, and sometimes it was terribly painful. However, after I had listened to Master Okawa's lecture, "The Mindset for Healing Illness" at Yufuin Shoshinkan on June 12, 2011, I felt my back getting warmer, then a dull pain and a grinding sensation. While I was in the bath that evening, I touched my spine and realized it had become straight.

(Woman, 50s, Kumamoto Prefecture)

My atopic dermatitis was healed!

In July 2008, I listened to the lecture, "How to Acquire Excellent Health" at a satellite venue. During the lecture, I felt the light of love and healing, and was embraced with a great sense of happiness. When I got home, I casually looked at myself in the mirror and saw that the dark red marks on my face caused by severe atopic dermatitis was healed clean.

(Woman, 50s, Mie Prefecture)

My terminal breast cancer disappeared!

In June 2008, I was told that I had terminal cancer and only four months left to live. I listened to Master Okawa's lecture, and was convinced that my own mind had created the cancer. So, I was determined to cure it with the power of my mind. I practiced self-reflection, gave gratitude, lived healthily, and offered prayers. Then, the 9-cm (3½-in) cancer started to shrink, and when I took "Prayer to Eradicate Cancer Cells," my medical test results showed that the cancer cells had clearly disappeared.

(Woman, 50s, Kanagawa Prefecture)

Ryuho Okawa's Series On Wellness and Healing Illness

Healing Power
The True Mechanism of Mind and Illness
[Tokyo: HS Press, 2016]

Miraculous Ways to Conquer Cancer
Awaken to the Power of Healing Within You
[Tokyo: HS Press, 2015]

Healing from Within
Life-Changing Keys to Calm, Spiritual, and Healthy Living
[New York: IRH Press, 2017]

The Manifesto of the Happiness Realization Party will dismiss Marx's Communist Manifesto and bring happiness

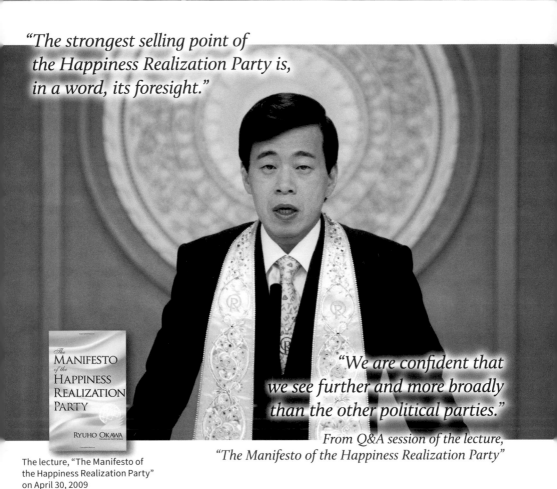

"The strongest selling point of the Happiness Realization Party is, in a word, its foresight."

"We are confident that we see further and more broadly than the other political parties."

From Q&A session of the lecture,
"The Manifesto of the Happiness Realization Party"

The lecture, "The Manifesto of the Happiness Realization Party" on April 30, 2009

Master Okawa, who had been giving spiritual teachings that lead people to happiness and giving political guidelines to the government, founded the Happiness Realization Party in May 2009. Just as he had announced in his lecture, "The Principle of Love" in 1987, he launched activities in many different fields to make people happy. In "The Manifesto of the Happiness Realization Party," the lecture he gave when the party was founded, he stated that his reason for going into politics was to make people happy,

Self-Defense Issue

HRP advocating since 2009

Warning about Chinese and North Korean threat!

When the HRP was founded in 2009, the dangers of China and North Korea were not yet fully recognized. The Japanese government and mass media even referred to North Korean missiles as "projectiles." However, the Happiness Realization Party quickly identified the military threat posed by China and North Korea, and proclaimed the need to strengthen Japan's national defense.

NHK News Apr. 5, 2009

(Broken link)
https://www.youtube.com/watch?v=BBTLUl4rJQo

Realized in 2010

Japan begins to strengthen its defense!

The threat posed by China and North Korea became an issue after the fishing boat collision near the Senkaku Islands in 2010 and the many North Korean missile launches and nuclear tests since 2014. The Japanese government is taking steps to strengthen national defense, the exercise of our right to collective self-defense has been approved, and Japan is now on its way to possess aircraft carriers.

(R) *The Tokyo Shimbun* published an article on Japan's need for aircraft carriers as self-defense. (December 18, 2018 issue)

(L) *The Sankei Shimbun* published an article regarding the revisions of the security bill and the right to collective self-defense. (March 29, 2016 issue)

and that the party is a movement completely opposite of The Communist Manifesto which has brought unhappiness to the world through materialism. This was the start of the activity "to recognize the existence of Buddha and God, and to create a utopian society." In the following decade, the Happiness Realization Party has led public opinion and worked day and night to make Japan capable of fighting against the hegemonic Chinese Communist Party.

Nuclear Power Issue

HRP advocating since 2011

Advocating the need for nuclear power!

As a result of the Japanese mass media's reports on the 2011 Great East Japan Earthquake, the public opinion turned completely toward abandoning nuclear power, and in 2012, all of Japan's 50 nuclear power plants were shut down. However, HRP has been insisting the need for nuclear power since a few days after the disaster, saying that it is dangerous for a country with poor energy resources to halt its nuclear power plants.

The suspension of all nuclear power generation meant that Japan had the lowest energy self-sufficiency rate out of all major countries!

90.8%

56.5% 60.3%

6.0%

Japan France UK USA

Realized in 2014

The government shifted its policy toward restarting the nuclear power plants!

As HRP continued to advocate the reactivation of nuclear power plants, the government began to shift its stance toward approving reactivation, and the Sendai Nuclear Power Plant in Kagoshima Prefecture resumed operation in 2015. Currently, nine nuclear power plants are in operation in Japan, and more than 10 additional plants are undergoing inspections for reactivation.

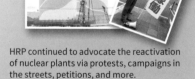

HRP continued to advocate the reactivation of nuclear plants via protests, campaigns in the streets, petitions, and more.

Into the Storm of International Politics:

The New Standards of the World Order

[Tokyo: HS Press, 2014]

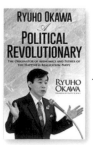

Ryuho Okawa
- A Political Revolutionary:

The Originator of Abenomics and Father of the Happiness Realization Party

[Tokyo: HS Press, 2014]

Economic Issue

HRP advocating since 2009

Announcing the measures against recession!

In the 2009 Japanese House of Representatives election, the HRP announced that its main policies were based on economic recovery, such as monetary easing, large-scale investment into infrastructure improvement among other things, and tax reduction and deregulation, and that the party's goal would be 3% annual inflation. The policies completely rejected the conventional wisdom of Japan's post-war economic policy, and presented a revolutionary strategy for growth.

HRP policy flyer, August 2019 issue

Realized in 2012

The Japanese government imitated the HRP policies, calling them "Abenomics"!

In December 2012, Prime Minister Abe announced his "Abenomics" which consisted of monetary easing, increased public spending on public works, and a strategy for growth via deregulation, etc. He imitated HRP's economic policies. However, he caused an economic downturn as a result of implementing a consumption tax hike, an idea opposed by HRP.

Happiness Realization Party has influenced Japanese politics

Ever since its founding in 2009, HRP has strongly insisted the enactment of an "anti-bullying law" to resolve bullying.

The Act for the Promotion of Measures to Prevent Bullying was enacted in 2013.

While the National Diet was divided and at a loss regarding the enactment of the Act on the Protection of Specially Designated Secrets, Master Okawa insisted in December 2013 that legislation is required in order to protect Japanese people from Chinese threat.

The Act on the Protection of Specially Designated Secrets was enacted in December 2014.

Timeline of
the Happiness Realization Party
and
the Japanese public opinion

Apr. 5, 2009 — North Korean missiles fly over the Japanese islands, but the government refers to them as "projectiles" and avoids making an official statement.

May 23, 2009 — The Happiness Realization Party (HRP) is founded. It fields 337 candidates in the House of Representatives election in August, advocating policies such as strengthening national defense and cutting taxes.

The Manifesto of the Happiness Realization Party
[Tokyo: HS Press, 2014]

Sep. 16, 2009 — The Democratic Party of Japan (DPJ) becomes the ruling party.

Master Okawa predicts in his lectures and spiritual messages that DPJ will increase taxes and cause a defense crisis. Following that, HRP begins the campaign to defeat DPJ.

Sep. 7, 2010 — A Chinese fishing boat rams a Japan Coast Guard patrol boat near the Senkaku Islands in Okinawa Prefecture.

HRP fields a candidate in the Okinawa gubernatorial election as the only party to advocate the relocation of the Futenma military base within Okinawa, to prepare against Chinese threat.

An urgent spiritual message from Amaterasu-O-Mikami, urging the government to resign and warning that divine punishment is imminent.

Mar. 11, 2011 — The Great East Japan Earthquake

The Naoto Kan administration requests the Hamaoka Nuclear Power Plant be shut down. This accelerates the movement to shut down nuclear power plants. Entire Japan becomes anti-nuclear.

May 9, 2011

▼

HRP launches the campaign to reactivate nuclear power plants and promote nuclear power generation.

Prime Minister Noda submits a proposal to the Tax Commission to increase consumption tax to 8% in 2014 and 10% in 2015.

December 2011

DPJ suffers a crushing defeat in the general election. Japan returns to conservatism after the Liberal Democratic Party (LDP) becomes the ruling party for the first time in three years.

December 2012

HRP's continuous call for the reactivation of nuclear power plants succeeds. The government changes its policy and approves the reactivation. The Sendai Nuclear Power Plant resumes operation in 2015, becoming the first to be reactivated since the disaster.

Apr. 11, 2014

Master Okawa records a spiritual message from the guardian spirit of Donald Trump, who was regarded as a fringe candidate, and predicts that he will be elected president.

January 2016

The Trump Secret:
Seeing Through the Past, Present, and
Future of the New American President
[New York: IRH Press, 2017]

▼

▼

Inauguration of Mr. Trump as the U.S. president.

January 2017

North Korea begins to test its missiles almost every month.

February 2017~

Master Okawa gives a lecture in Berlin, Germany, criticizing the Chinese government's human rights suppression of Uyghurs and other ethnic groups.

Oct. 7, 2018

Love for the Future
[New York: IRH Press, 2019]

▼

▼

The Chinese government acknowledges the existence of concentration camps for Uyghurs.

Oct. 17, 2018

A spiritual message from Mao Zedong, China's founding father, reveals the hidden darkness at the root of Chinese hegemonism.

November 2018

Realizing an ideal education, a long-term national plan, the founding of Happy Science Academy

"I want Happy Science to raise the banner of religious education and engage in educational activities such as running schools and Buddha's Truth prep schools."

From the lecture, "On School Education and Freedom of Devils"

Seeing cases of bullying in schools getting worse and the schools concealing them, Master Okawa gave a series of lectures on education from December 2006. The following year, he proposed a bill to punish bullying, and six years after that, in 2013, the Act for the Promotion of Measures to Prevent Bullying was enacted by the National Diet.

Moreover, he sought to create the ideal education based on faith which would build individuals with noble character, and planned to establish the Happy Science Academy Junior and Senior High School. The Nasu Main Campus opened in 2010 and the Kansai Campus in 2013. The two schools are continuing to do well, both in academic performance and extracurricular activities. Our movement to reform education, which is regarded as a long-term national plan, is steadily becoming a reality.

In the March 2007 issue of *The Liberty*, Master Okawa proposed a special bill about the punishment for bullying. Six years later, the Act for the Promotion of Measures to Prevent Bullying was enacted in June 2013.

For more on *The Liberty*, visit: http://eng.the-liberty.com/

2007 Special proposal for a bill to punish bullying, and supporting an NPO

Network to Protect Children from Bullying

Master Okawa called for the need to legislate an anti-bullying law to resolve the issue of bullying, and in the March 2007 issue of The Liberty, published a special proposal for a bill to punish bullying. Six years later, in June 2013, the Japanese government established the Act for the Promotion of Measures to Prevent Bullying. Meanwhile, in February 2007, Happy Science began its support for the NPO, Network to Protect Children from Bullying (established February 2007). The NPO has consulted more than 8,000 cases of bullying and helped resolve 90% of them.

2010 The opening of Happy Science Academy Nasu Main Campus

Tochigi Prefecture approved the establishment of Happy Science Academy on December 1, 2009. In April 2010, its Nasu Main Campus opened in the grounds of Happy Science Head Temple Nasu Shoja. The boarding-type, combined junior and senior high school offers high-level intellectual training and moral education. With this, we began to train future leaders who will contribute to society.

2013 The opening of Happy Science Academy Kansai Campus

Kansai Campus in Otsu, Shiga Prefecture opened in April 2013. Like the Nasu Main Campus, it is a combined junior and senior high school. Its focus also includes educating future entrepreneurs and medical professionals.

Happy Science Academy Nasu Main Campus
Opened in 2010

Happy Science Academy has posted excellent achievements ever since its opening. Students not only pass university entrance exams and English proficiency tests, but also perform brilliantly in extracurricular activities. One such example is the junior high school cheerleading team's victory in the world championship in 2016.

Happy Science Academy Kansai Campus
Opened in 2013

Achievements of Happy Science Academy
(# of students who passed their university entrance exams in 2019, both campuses combined)

Happy Science University: 135, The University of Tokyo: 3, Kyoto University: 1, Waseda University: 14, Keio University: 4, etc.

Junior high school cheerleading team won the world championship (2016), and more.

Creation of Happy Science University, the base of a new civilization

"HSU is also the source of a new civilization.
Here, we can find the mainstream thought
of an educational revolution that will start from Japan."

From the lecture, "Challenge into the Unknown"

Master Okawa revealed his plan for Happy Science University in April 2012, in a lecture entitled, "Happy Science University and the Future Society."

Following Happy Science Academy, Happy Science University (HSU) opened in Chosei, Chiba Prefecture on April 1, 2015 as an institute for higher religious research run by Happy Science.

HSU is working to integrate today's highly specialized and complex academic disciplines under Buddha's Truth, which brings happiness to all people, and to become a university where new branches of learning are created. It will be the foundation for creating the future of Japan and the base from which a new civilization will be transmitted: HSU was established as the dream and hope of the entire world.

Classes in session at Happy Science University.

Four Highly Creative and Practical Faculties

Faculty of Human Happiness

Pursuing human studies to become the leaders who will open a new era

Students research deeply into the essence of humanity and true happiness, with a main focus on Happy Science teachings. They study humanities, including philosophy, theology and psychology, and the faculty produces cultured graduates with advanced linguistic skills who will become leaders or religious professionals capable of playing an active role on the global stage.

Faculty of Successful Management

Raising entrepreneurs who can bring success to their company and prosperity to their country

In addition to conventional management studies, students study Happy Science teachings on management and success that lead them to produce wealth and prosperity. They also study law and economics to develop their ability to solve real issues in society. The faculty aims to produce talented graduates who can contribute to the world.

Faculty of Future Industry

Taking up the challenge of creating the source of a new civilization

The core focus is on mechanical, electronic and information engineering, and students acquire extensive learning about cutting-edge technology in fields such as the physical sciences and space engineering. They refine their entrepreneurial spirit by also learning about technology management, boost their creativity and imagination by studying Happy Science teachings, and pioneer future industries.

Faculty of Future Creation

Nurturing leading figures who will change the times and create the future

Students study political science, journalism, performing arts, artistic expression, and more, and explore and transmit new political and cultural models based on "truth, goodness and beauty." They research how to capture people's hearts and minds, and develop into human resources with virtue who play an active role in many different fields.

HSU's Faculty of Future Creation Tokyo Campus was completed in March 2017. Undergraduates in the Faculty of Future Creation study here.

For more information, please visit: http://happy-science.university/en/

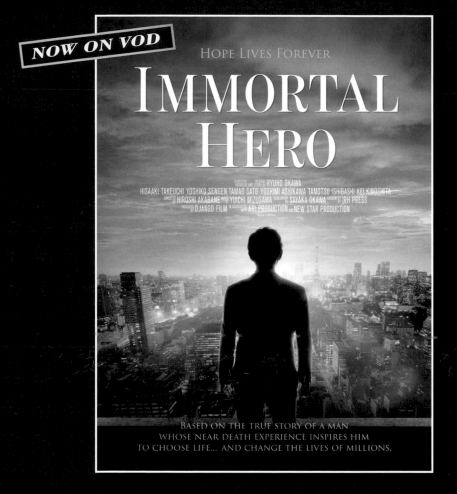

Movie Awards from Around the World

Happy Science movies that have been produced by the Executive Producer Master Ryuho Okawa are receiving many awards worldwide and below are a few photos taken at the award ceremonies. The movies that illustrate the truth of life are moving many people worldwide.

Executive Producer and Original Story
By Master Ryuho Okawa

29 Awards from 6 Countries!

WINNER
BEST DIRECTOR
OF A FOREIGN LANGUAGE
FEATURE FILM
MADRID
2019

The awards are all the works of the Executive Producer Master Ryuho Okawa. It has been my dream to offer the trophies of Happy Science movies to Master Okawa.
Director Hiroshi Akabane

Oct. 15th - 20th

At San Diego International Film Festival, the movie was played and the main characters Hisaaki Takeuchi and Kei Kinoshita talked about the highlights of the movie.

Oct. 14th

In Los Angeles, producer Hisaaki Takeuchi spoke about the key impressions of the movie.

WORLD PREMIERE AWARD NOMINATION

OFFICIAL SELECTION
SAN DIEGO INTERNATIONAL FILM FESTIVAL

Merit Award
Awareness
Film Festival
2019

http://immortal-hero.com/ **ENTER**

Oct. 15th

Movie **The Laws of the Universe** – Part I

7 Awards from 4 Countries!

First Showing in Israel!

The movie was shown to the audience at Icon Festival in Tel Aviv, Israel.

HOUSTON INTERNATIONAL
FILM FESTIVAL
ANIMATION AWARD
SILVER AWARD

NICE INTERNATIONAL
FILM FESTIVAL 2019
BEST INTERNATIONAL
ANIMATION AWARD

...and many more.

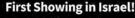

https://laws-of-universe.hspicturesstudio.com/ **ENTER**

As of December 12, 2019

Our award-winning movies offer views on people and the world that make people happy

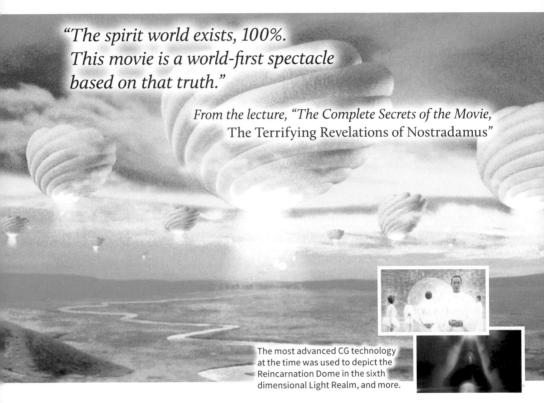

"The spirit world exists, 100%. This movie is a world-first spectacle based on that truth."

From the lecture, "The Complete Secrets of the Movie, The Terrifying Revelations of Nostradamus"

The most advanced CG technology at the time was used to depict the Reincarnation Dome in the sixth dimensional Light Realm, and more.

The movie *The Terrifying Revelations of Nostradamus* was released on September 10, 1994. Since then, 17 more movies have been produced and planned by Master Okawa. These movies offer views on people and the world which bring them happiness. Each release draws an even wider audience, and the highly-regarded movies have won various awards in Japan and the world.

Starting with the first movie in 1994, we originally made and released one movie every three years, but we picked up the pace year after year since Master Okawa's new resurrection in 2004. There were a few cases when we released as many as three movies in a year. Our movies are also making incredible progress beyond worldly common sense, in both quality and quantity.

Movies and Awards

1994 **The Terrifying Revelations of Nostradamus** (live action)
Asahi Best 10 Film Festival Top Prize in Readers' Award (1995), and more.

1997 **Love Blows Like the Wind** (animation)
Mainichi Film Award for Animation Film Second Place, and more.

2000 **The Laws of the Sun** (animation)
Asahi Best 10 Film Festival Top Prize in Readers' Award (2001), and more.

2003 **The Golden Laws** (animation)

2006 **The Laws of Eternity** (animation)

2009 **The Rebirth of Buddha** (animation)

2012 **The Final Judgement** (live action)
A Selected Film for Japan-Filmfest Hamburg

The Mystical Laws (animation)
Special Jury Award at the 46th WorldFest Houston International Film Festival /
"Palm Beach International Film Festival" Nominated for Best Feature Official Selection /
"Monstra, the Lisbon Animated Film Festival" /
"Japan-Filmfest Hamburg" Official Selection /
"Buddhist Film Festival Europe" Official Selection /
Asian Film Festival of Dallas" Official selection /
"Proctors 4th Annual Animation Festival" Official Selection, and more

2015 **The Laws of the Universe - Part 0** (animation)
Nominated in the 10th Dingle International Film Festival for "ANIMATION DINGLE: Animated Feature Film" /
Screened at Czech Republic 15th annual Animefest /
Grand Jury Prize – Best Anime Feature at Film Invasion Los Angeles

2016 **I'm Fine, My Angel** (live action)

2017 **The World We Live In** (live action)
Best Feature Award International New York Film Festival 2017, and more.

2018 **Heart to Heart** (documentary)
Best Documentary Feature Film-International /
Hollywood Verge Film Awards /
Award of Merit at The Indel FEST Film Awards

DAYBREAK (live action)

The Laws of the Universe - Part I (animation)
Special Jury Animation Award at the Awareness Film Festival /
Outstanding Achievement Award at the Calcutta International Cult Film Festival /
Grand Jury Prize – Best Anime Feature at Film Invasion Los Angeles /
Best Animated Film Award at the Nice International Film Festival /
Best International Animation Feature Film Award at the London International Motion Picture Awards /
Silver Remi at the 52nd Annual WorldFest Houston International Film Festival

2019 **The Last White Witch** (live action)

Life is Beautiful - Heart to Heart 2 - (documentary)

Immortal Hero (live action)
The Castell Award at Barcelona International Film Festival 2019 /
Winner of July 2019 Indie Visions Film Festival/
Winner July 2019 of Diamond Film Awards /
The Best Original Screenplay and honorable mention at Florence Film Awards /
Winner of Best Foreign Language Feature Film and Official Selection in Madrid International Film Festival

2020 **The Real Exorcist** (live action)

The Laws of the Universe - Part I

NICE INTERNATIONAL
REMI SPECIAL JURY AWARD

LONDON INTERNATIONAL MOTION
BEST INTERNATIONAL ANIMATION
FEATURE FILM AWARD

The Mystical Laws

46TH WORLDFEST HOUSTON
INTERNATIONAL FILM FESTIVAL
PICTURE AWARDS FESTIVAL
REMI SPECIAL JURY AWARD

Blowing away the darkness in entertainment and bringing light, love, and truth to the whole world

"Stars and entertainers need to be aware of their responsibility that they are steadily influencing the way people lead their lives."

From the lecture, "Buddha's Truth Will Open a New Age of Entertainment"

Yoshiko Sengen of ARI Production performs "Yume no Jikan" (Dreamtime), the image song for *The Last White Witch*.

Master Ryuho Okawa established the Future Stars Training Department in 2008 and the New Star Production entertainment agency in 2011. As the movie industry evolves, he wants to produce many actors and entertainers who express the Truth. He recorded a series of spiritual messages from spirits associated with entertainment, and gave a string of lectures intended to guide the entertainment industry in the right direction.

Fumika Shimizu (Japanese actress, religious name: Yoshiko Sengen) sparked a media uproar when she renounced the world and became a staff of Happy Science in 2017. This cast a light upon the darkness in the Japanese entertainment industry and triggered internal and external movements to purify the entertainment world. Meanwhile, Master Okawa established another agency, ARI Production, in 2017. We are conducting entertainment activities that bring joy and happiness to people.

Dance Performance

Acting Lessons

Future Stars Training Department

Founded in 2008 with the goal to produce star missionaries, such as artists, actors, models, dancers, voice actors, and entertainers who will play an active role in entertainment and bring love to the world.

Entertainment activities have been in full motion since 2011

NEW STAR
PRODUCTION

New Star Production Co., Ltd.

Established in January 2011 as the entertainment agency of the Happy Science Group. Master Okawa was appointed chairman of New Star Production in January 2016. Reborn, it is now in full motion with projects such as movies, TV shows and plays.

ARI Production

ARI Production Co., Ltd.

Established in 2016 as the entertainment planning department of Happy Science. Master Okawa was appointed chairman of ARI Production in May 2017. The two entertainment agencies have been launched, and they are in friendly competition to further polish their entertainment activities.

Over 100 lyrics and songs created by Master Okawa

RYUHO OKAWA ALL TIME BEST I&II
Lyrics and songs written
by Ryuho Okawa

Master Okawa writes many lyrics and songs for Happy Science through inspiration from the heavenly world. He has composed more than 100 of them, including theme songs and insert songs for our movies. His compositions cover a wide range of genres, including songs for pep rallies and school songs for Happy Science Academy and Happy Science University.

More and more miracles are working with every chance

Ritual Prayer

Eyesight recovered in my left eye!

I had been having trouble with my left eye since last October. I couldn't focus, and I was seeing double. However, when I took "Prayer to Restore Function," my entire body was filled with energy, and my eyesight recovered immediately after the prayer. (Female, 60s, Kanagawa Prefecture)

9-cm nails pierced into my head, but I survived safely thanks to prayer!

Two 9-cm (3½-in) nails pierced deep into my head due to the mishandling of a machine on the construction site. Unconscious, I was taken to a hospital, and the doctor told my family, "The chance of there being no aftereffects is zero. He will be brain dead after a brain hemorrhage." However, after the company chairman and president took ritual prayers such as "Super Strong Prayer for Recovery from Illness," I had no brain haemorrhage, and the operation was a success. There were no aftereffects, and I was able to return to work two months later. (Male, 40s, Kagoshima Prefecture)

Necrosis, a lost toe, and regeneration!

My husband suffers from severe diabetes. Last year, he was recommended a below-the-knee amputation due to the necrosis in his left ring toe. He took ritual prayers such as "Prayer to Eradicate Illness," and he gave deep gratitude to the Lord and reflected on himself every day. He had lost a part of his ring toe, below its joint, but it began to regenerate, and the toe returned to its original size in four months. He no longer needed the operation. "That's absolutely impossible!" was all that the doctor could say. (Female, 50s, Aichi Prefecture)

Movie

Completely recovered from a spinal disc herniation!

A while ago, I had persistent back pain from a slipped disc. One day, I went to watch the movie, *The Laws of the Universe -Part 0-* at a movie theater, even though I had a hard time simply staying seated. But after the movie, I realized that my back felt much better. When I watched it again, the back pain was totally gone; it was completely healed! It was astonishing. (Female, 50s, Kumamoto Prefecture)

Master's Lecture

Recovered from a severe case of alopecia areata!

I developed alopecia areata last October. At first, I developed a bald spot that was a few centimeters in diameter, but eventually, I lost around 80% of my hair. But when I attended Master Okawa's lecture, "The Power to Believe," my hair started to grow back that very same day. Now, I have a full head of hair. (Female, 40s, Oita Prefecture)

Sutra

An incurable illness was completely healed by reciting "The True Words Spoken By Buddha"!

In 2006, I was immediately hospitalized after being diagnosed with pneumonia. The doctor said I had episodic interstitial lung disease. It's an incurable disease with no known cause, and patients are expected to only live five to six years after contracting it. I was living at home until I could be transferred to a university hospital, during which time I recited, "The True Words Spoken By Buddha" (Japanese version) every morning and every night. I also reflected on my human relationships. A week later, the doctor examined me again and was surprised to find that my condition was improving. I continued to recite the sutra, and when the doctor examined me again a week later, he was absolutely stunned to find that I had completely recovered! (Male, 60s, Tokushima Prefecture)

The Gold Powder Phenomenon

Gold powder falling at lecture venues

In a lecture entitled, "The Power to Make Miracles" in December 2018, Master Okawa proclaimed that, from then on, Happy Science will be seeing more miracles than ever before. Just as he said, gold powder fell near the lecture stage (Makuhari Messe in Chiba Prefecture).

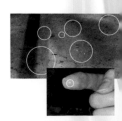

Natural Disaster

The tsunami bypassed Chiba Shoshinkan!

The Pacific coast of Chiba suffered damage by the 2011 Great East Japan Earthquake. Many homes were completely destroyed or flooded by the tremors and tsunamis. A major warning of a 10-m (33-ft) high tsunami was issued for Chosei-mura in Chiba. However, the tsunami bypassed Chosei-mura, the village where Happy Science Chiba Shoshinkan stands. The tsunami did not reach the coastlines near Chiba Shoshinkan; the temple is just a five-minute walk away from the coastline. This shows that having a Happy Science temple mitigates the level of disaster.

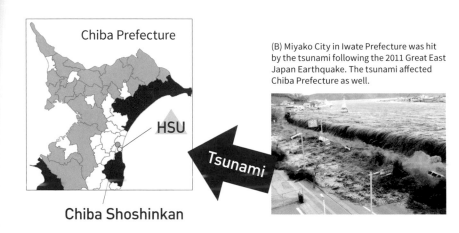

Chiba Prefecture

HSU

Tsunami

Chiba Shoshinkan

(B) Miyako City in Iwate Prefecture was hit by the tsunami following the 2011 Great East Japan Earthquake. The tsunami affected Chiba Prefecture as well.

An inscribed monument of gratitude was built in the grounds of Chiba Shoshinkan in January 2013 to tell future generations about the tsunami-repelling miracle.

Chiba Shoshinkan

Sanjo Temple in Niigata

Ms. Keiko Tateiri and followers of Sanjo Temple

I went to my local temple and practiced self-reflection and prayer every week. Then, my cervical cancer disappeared!

This April, I was diagnosed with cervical cancer. I was so shocked that I immediately went to Sanjo Local Temple. The temple manager listened to me caringly and gave me advice on healing the illness, and also recommended me to take ritual prayers. Then, the temple manager and members gathered in the prayer room to pray for my recovery. When I was reciting the prayers, I was embraced by the Lord's light and felt happy, and tears started to well up. I thought, "What is this warm feeling?" After that, I went to the local temple every week, and practiced self-reflection and prayer. I also read Master's book, *Cho Zettai Kenkoho* [lit. "The Way to Definite Health"](Tokyo: IRH Press, 2009). In Chapter 3, it says that illnesses related to female organs such as breast cancer and cervical cancer result from relationship issues between husband and wife.

When I looked into my mind, I found that I was getting irritated by small things and fighting with my husband over them. However, my husband was studying about my illness and praying for me to get better. When I saw him do that, I tried to remember and reflect on all the things he had done for me. I discovered so many things that I took for granted and did not thank him for.

As I repeatedly went to the local temple, my self-reflection progressed well, and as my gratitude toward my husband deepened, I naturally became kinder.

Then, when I went for a check-up three weeks later, the cancer was gone! The nurse asked, "How did the cancer disappear? Did you eat a certain kind of food?" I am thankful for this miracle, and will continue to spread the Truth.

Master's Lectures Have Been Changing the World

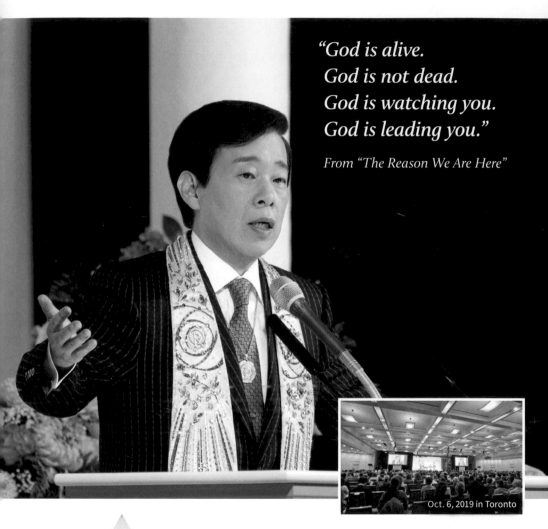

"God is alive.
God is not dead.
God is watching you.
God is leading you."

From *"The Reason We Are Here"*

Oct. 6, 2019 in Toronto

MIRACULOUS
MILESTONE
3000
MASTER RYUHO OKAWA
OVER 3,000 LECTURES!!

Master's overseas missionary tour began on Nov. 18, 2007 in Hawaii, with the most recent tour being his trip to Toronto in 2019. His lectures have been influencing and changing the world.

(A) Oct. 2, 2016 in New York

(L) Taken on May 21. An audience of 6,000 in the Philippines.

(A) Taken on Jun. 23, 2012. An audience of 10,000 in Uganda.

(L) Taken on Nov. 6, 2011. An audience of 13,000 in Sri Lanka.
(B) Taken on Mar. 6, 2011. An audience of 40,000 in Bodh Gaya, India.

A Record of Master's Missionary Tour to the Five Continents

Canada

USA

Brazil

1 Nov. 18, 2007 Hawaii
BE POSITIVE

2 Mar. 21, 2008 San Francisco
ON HAPPINESS

3 Mar. 23, 2008 Los Angeles
HAPPY ATTITUDE

4 Sep. 28, 2008 New York
THE WAY TO SUCCESS

5 Oct. 2, 2016 New York
FREEDOM, JUSTICE, AND HAPPINESS

6 Oct. 6, 2019 Toronto
THE REASON WE ARE HERE

7 Jul. 27, 2008 London
WHAT IS REAL LIFE?

8 Oct. 7, 2018 Berlin
LOVE FOR THE FUTURE

9 Nov. 7, 2010 Sao Paulo
ON MYSTICAL POWER

10 Nov. 9, 2010 Sorocaba
THE POWER OF INVINCIBLE THINKING

11 Nov. 10, 2010 Jundiai
THE WAY TO HAPPINESS

12 Nov. 12, 2010 Sao Paulo
AWAKENING TO THE TRUTH

13 Nov. 14, 2010 Sao Paulo
LOVE AND WORK OF ANGELS

14 Jun. 23, 2012 Kampala
THE LIGHT OF NEW HOPE

15 Mar. 29, 2009 Sydney
YOU CAN BE THE PERSON YOU WANT TO BECOME

16 Oct. 14, 2012 Sydney
ASPIRATIONS FOR THE FUTURE WORLD

*"I have already abandoned my earthly life.
My sole desire is to spread this Truth to the end of the world.
I just want you to follow me and spread these teachings
to every corner of the world."*

From The Laws of Salvation

U.K.
7 8
Germany

South Korea
17

Nepal
20 23
22
India
21

Taiwan
18 19
25
Hong Kong

24
The Philippines

Sri Lanka 28 27
26
Malaysia
Singapore

14
Uganda

Australia
15 16

17 Jun. 15, 2008 Seoul
BELIEVING IN EACH OTHER

18 Nov. 9, 2008 Taipei
**THE REALIZATION OF
BUDDHALAND UTOPIA**

19 Mar. 3, 2019 Taipei
LOVE SURPASSES HATRED

20 Feb. 27, 2011 Delhi
FAITH AND LOVE

21 Mar. 2, 2011 Mumbai
HOW TO SUCCEED IN LIFE

22 Mar. 6, 2011 Bodh Gaya
**THE REAL BUDDHA AND
NEW HOPE**

23 Mar. 4, 2011 Kathmandu
LIFE AND DEATH

24 May 21, 2011 Antipolo
LOVE AND SPIRITUAL POWER

25 May 22, 2011 Hong Kong
THE FACT AND THE TRUTH

26 Sep. 15, 2011 Singapore
HAPPINESS AND PROSPERITY

27 Sep. 18, 2011 Kuala Lumpur
THE AGE OF MERCY

28 Nov. 6, 2011 Sri Jayawardenepura Kotte
**THE POWER OF NEW
ENLIGHTENMENT**

Some of Master's Impacts On the World

The New York lecture influenced the U.S. presidential election

In his lecture on Oct. 2, 2016, Master Okawa stated that the next president should be Donald Trump, and Trump eventually made a comeback victory.

Master Okawa's lectures broadcasted in the U.S.

In 2016, just before his missionary tour to New York, Master Okawa's lectures were broadcasted on FOX 5, an affiliate of one of the four major American networks, Fox. The program, "Invitation to Happiness" aired for eight weeks.

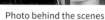

Photo behind the scenes

"Invitation to Happiness" aired on FOX 5

You can watch all episodes of "Invitation to Happiness" on YouTube:
https://www.youtube.com/channel/UCBX_lW-_rYBrGnDcjhZ3USw

The Hong Kong lecture led people to the Umbrella Revolution

In his 2011 Hong Kong missionary tour, Master Okawa gave a message to "Hong Kong-ize" China. Three years later, the Umbrella Revolution occurred.

Abante News reporting about the lecture in Antipolo, the Philippines

(Uganda) The Observer printed an article with the headline, "Happy Science founder brings hope to Ugandans."

(Africa) In total, more than 30 million people watched the lecture in Uganda through TV broadcast.

Age News reporting about the lecture in Bodh Gaya, India

(Nepal) Gorkhapatra: "Happy Science Master and Happiness Realization Party President Ryuho Okawa gave a lecture in Kathmandu. (...) Japan's national teacher, Master Okawa, has given more than 1,400 lectures to date."

(Sri Lanka) Master's lecture was broadcasted live and uncut on three TV stations. Northern Indian newspaper Aaj wrote that Sri Lanka has accepted the rebirth of Buddha on their front page.

Happy Science Charities Around the World

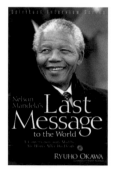

HS Nelson Mandela Fund was established as an internal fund of the Happy Science Group following the publication of *Nelson Mandela's Last Message to the World*, a book of spiritual message from the late Nelson Mandela. The fund provides material and spiritual aid to those who suffer from racial discrimination, poverty, political oppression, natural disasters and so on. Children and young people around the world are also presented with opportunities to receive education through this fund.

NEPAL:
After the 2015 Nepal Earthquake, Happy Science promptly offered its Nepal Local Temple as a temporary evacuation center and utilized its global network to send such relief supplies as water, food, and tents. Recovery of Nepal has been supported through HS Nelson Mandela Fund. (Photo 1) In addition, in collaboration with the Nepalese Ambassador to Japan, profit from the screening of *The Rebirth of Buddha*, a movie produced by the Happy Science Group, was offered to build schools and provide educational support in Nepal, the birthplace of Buddha.

SRI LANKA:
Happy Science provided aid in construction of school buildings damaged by the Tsunami. One hundred bookshelves were donated to Buddhist temples with the help of the Sri Lankan prime minister.

INDIA:
HS Nelson Mandela Fund has been supporting schools in Bodh Gaya, a sacred ground of Buddhism. Medical aid was offered in Kolkata, in collaboration with local hospitals.

CHINA:
Financial support and donation of tents were made to the Szechuan Earthquake disaster zone. Also, books were donated to elementary schools in Gansu Province near the disaster zone.

MALAYSIA:
Financial aid and donation of educational materials and clothes to local orphanages were made. Relief supplies were sent to the site of the 2015 floods in northeast Malaysia.

THAILAND:
Happy Science constructed libraries and donated books for elementary and junior high schools damaged by floods in Ayutthaya.

INDONESIA:
Donation was made to the Sumatra-Andaman Earthquake disaster zone.

THE PHILIPPINES:
Books and electric fans were donated to elementary schools in Leyte Island in July 2015. Five thousand sets of health and hygiene kits were donated after the Typhoon Haiyan (Yolanda).

UGANDA:
Mosquito nets and educational materials were donated to protect children from Malaria. Scholarships were offered to orphans diagnosed with AIDS.

On February 15, 2018, a classroom building and a prayer hall opened in the grounds of St. Mary's Secondary School in Kampala, Uganda. The boards on the sides are dedicated to Happy Science and the Nelson Mandela Foundation. This was made possible through the joint efforts of HS Nelson Mandela Fund and the Nelson Mandela Foundation, which is an organization that takes on the legacy of the former South African President Nelson Mandela.

KENYA:
English version of *Invincible Thinking*, *An Unshakable Mind*, and *The Laws of Success* were donated to schools. Those books were designated as supplementary texts by the Kenyan Ministry of Education in 2014.

GHANA:
Medical supplies were donated as a preventive measure against Ebola.

SOUTH AFRICA:
In collaboration with Nelson Mandela Foundation, a container library and books were donated to an elementary school in South Africa. (Photo 2)

AUSTRALIA:
In 2011, donation was made to the flood-affected northeastern area via the Australian Embassy in Japan.

NEW ZEALAND:
In February 2011, donation was made to the earthquake-stricken area via the New Zealand Embassy in Japan.

IRAN:
In October 2012, donation was made to the earthquake-stricken area in northeastern Iran via the Iranian Embassy in Japan.

BRAZIL:
Donation was made to the flood-affected area in January 2011.

BENIN:
Constructed a borehole in an orphanage in Benin. (Photos 3&4)
Donated books, scholarships, stationery, and clothes to orphans in Benin.(Photo 5)

HAWAII:
"Prevention Against Suicide" rally in Kauai. (Photo 6)

We provide aid to many other countries, too. And utilize our global network to aid those who are unnoticed and unheard.

Master Okawa's foresight regarding the Trump Revolution, which is currently leading the world

With regard to the extremely chaotic situation inside and outside of Japan, Master Okawa continues to show the direction we should take from the perspective of God's plan for the world, as a world teacher. For example, predictions by the mass media and experts, in Japan and overseas, about matters such as the Trump Revolution currently leading the international affairs or the Brexit issue are missing their mark completely. However, through his lectures, spiritual messages, and writings, Master Okawa is showing the global community the true nature of these issues, how to resolve them, and the direction in which we should be moving. Many of the things he said have actually happened and are attracting a lot of attention. We will take a look at his predictions, the real facts, and his opinion after-the-fact.

2015 *Reality*

Dec. 15, 2015 From the lecture "To the World We Can Believe In":

"According to one type of calendar, 2016 is said to be a year of revolution."

Dec. 31, 2015 From the lecture "A Review of 2015 and the Outlook for 2016":

"I want to make 2016 a year brimming with hope. I expect it to be a year of revolution. I think that unexpected things will start to happen."

opinion

Jan. 9 From "The Lecture On *The Laws of Justice*":

"(The Japanese mass media and politicians) say that, since the magnitude of the earthquake was small, it was no different from an A-bomb, but you could say that, in a sense, it is very highly likely that they have successfully miniaturized the A-bomb."

Jun. 28, 1989 From the lecture "Revolutionizing Your Perspective":

"Donald Trump built a vast fortune at the age of 42 or 43. He's a skilled New York real estate tycoon who has enough energy to eventually aim for the U.S. presidency."

Written on Jan. 11, 2016 From *The Trump Secret: Seeing Through the Past, Present, and Future of the New American President*

"I hope he (Mr. Donald Trump) will be a great new leader of the U.S."
(From Preface for Chapter 4)

Jul. 12, 1994 From the lecture "Visiting Other Dimensions":

"North Korea already possesses nuclear weapons."

Mar. 13, 2016 From the lecture "The Power of Miracles That Can Change the Era" given in Fukuoka:

"This is the final warning. It might really be the last chance before everything is over. (...) Think hard about what is waiting for us in the future."

Prediction

comes true

comes true

Jan. 6
North Korea announces its first H-bomb experiment

Apr. 14
Over 150 people die in the Kumamoto earthquakes

2016

opinion

Apr. 15 From the spiritual message "Exploring God's Will in the Magnitude 7 Kumamoto Earthquake":

"(Divine Spirit:) When something like an earthquake, volcanic eruption or tsunami occurs, it means we are sending some kind of political message in it."

Opinion

Published Apr. 21, 2013 From the preface for *Guardian Spirit Interview: Questioning the Crown Prince about His Self-Awareness as the Next Emperor*:

"The current imperial family are the direct descendants of Amaterasu-O-Mikami, which means that they are of a special rank which differentiates them from ordinary citizens, so I think that their matters should not be discussed in a democratic way like the common people."

Prediction

Dec. 9, 1990 From the lecture "The Crusade for the Future":

"This integration of the European Community will surely fail. The first country to pull out will be the U.K."

Reality

comes true

Jul.20

The court of arbitration in The Hague does not acknowledge the rights in the South China Sea claimed by China

Aug. 8

Emperor Akihito expresses his wish to abdicate

Jun. 23

The U.K. decides to leave the EU

2016

Opinion

opinion

Dec. 7 From the lecture "The Way to the Truth":

"The imperial system in Japan does not exist simply as part of an organization or system. In truth, it exists as a religious means. (...) If His Imperial Majesty is wavering in his decision like how the president of a company would, (...) then they will be less respected by the people and the future of the imperial family may be in serious danger.

opinion

Jun. 25 From the lecture "Courageous Decisions":

"It is becoming extremely dangerous since the U.K.'s decision to withdraw means that there is the possibility of other countries following suit."

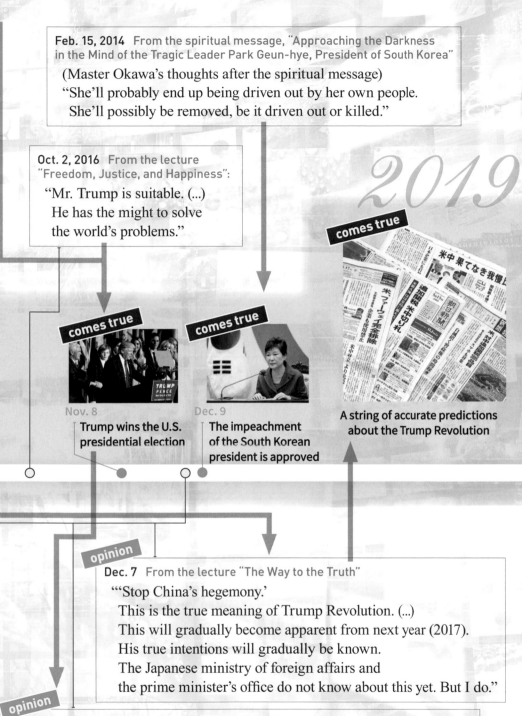

Feb. 15, 2014 From the spiritual message, "Approaching the Darkness in the Mind of the Tragic Leader Park Geun-hye, President of South Korea"

(Master Okawa's thoughts after the spiritual message)
"She'll probably end up being driven out by her own people.
She'll possibly be removed, be it driven out or killed."

Oct. 2, 2016 From the lecture "Freedom, Justice, and Happiness":

"Mr. Trump is suitable. (...)
He has the might to solve
the world's problems."

2019

comes true

comes true

comes true

Nov. 8
Trump wins the U.S. presidential election

Dec. 9
The impeachment of the South Korean president is approved

A string of accurate predictions about the Trump Revolution

opinion

Dec. 7 From the lecture "The Way to the Truth"

"'Stop China's hegemony.'
This is the true meaning of Trump Revolution. (...)
This will gradually become apparent from next year (2017).
His true intentions will gradually be known.
The Japanese ministry of foreign affairs and
the prime minister's office do not know about this yet. But I do."

opinion

Dec. 7 From the lecture "The Way to the Truth"

"In regards to this year's election, our headquarters in North America
worked really hard. (...) So, what I said last year about using our strength
to make this year a year of revolution has actually taken shape on the
global level before it took place in Japan."

Various space people influence Earth. We investigate their objectives and explore the mission of earthlings.

"A journey has now begun to explore where the souls of earthlings came from.

This work will also foretell how the civilization of Earth should be in the future."

From the afterword for Space-People Readings

Space-people reading by Master Ryuho Okawa on March 16, 2010 at Happy Science General Headquaters, Tokyo.

Master Okawa began conducting space-people readings in 2010 to explore the reality of UFOs (unidentified flying objects) and extraterrestrials seen all over the world.

As a result, we have learned the objectives of space people coming to Earth. They are very interested in Earth because it's the ideal spiritual training ground for the soul, and it has become clear that there are space people of evil nature plotting to invade Earth.

Happy Science is amassing information on space people that even the "leading intelligence" on UFOs such as the U.S. and European countries are unaware of, so now, Japan is about to grow out of its shell as a "developing intelligence" on UFOs. Also, Master Okawa began conducting UFO readings in 2018, and we are starting to see a new connection between the universe and the Spirit World.

What we found through space-people readings

Objective 1
Defend Earth

Various space people have formed an alliance to protect the spiritual training ground known as Earth. They are making every effort to prevent wars and invasions by malignant space people.

Objective 2
Learn the teachings of the God of Earth

Many space people listen to the teachings of the God of Earth El Cantare and relay them back to their mother planet. A diversity of space people have migrated to Earth to learn the teachings of love by the God of Earth.

Objective 3
Migrate to Earth

Since billions of years ago, space people have flown to Earth and been reborn on Earth over and over again. Between 30 and 40% of the Earth's population are earthlings who have the souls of those space people, and so far as many as 500 species of space people have been discovered.

Objective 4
Investigate Earth

A number of space people are investigating the ecology of earthlings. It has been proven that they carry out abductions and perform experiments on living people.

Objective 5
Invade Earth

Malignant Reptilians (reptile-like space people) exist who are scheming to use earthlings as their food. It is now clear that they are currently manipulating the leader of China.

Alien Invasion: Can We Defend Earth?
[Tokyo: HS Press, 2015]

UFOs Caught on Camera!: A Spiritual Investigation on Videos and Photos of the Luminous Objects Visiting Earth
[Tokyo: HS Press, 2018]

Breaking the Silence: Interviews with Space People
[Available only in main and local temples, and branches of Happy Science. Refer to the contact information.]

We are not alone in this Universe
[Available only in main and local temples, and branches of Happy Science. Refer to the contact information.]

In preparation of the coming *space age*—where humans will come in contact with space people—Master Okawa began conducting space-people readings in 2010. He has examined and published key information, such as the cultures of different planets and the technology behind UFO flight. What is this ability of the spiritual readings of Master Okawa? Let's take a look at the secret behind the readings.

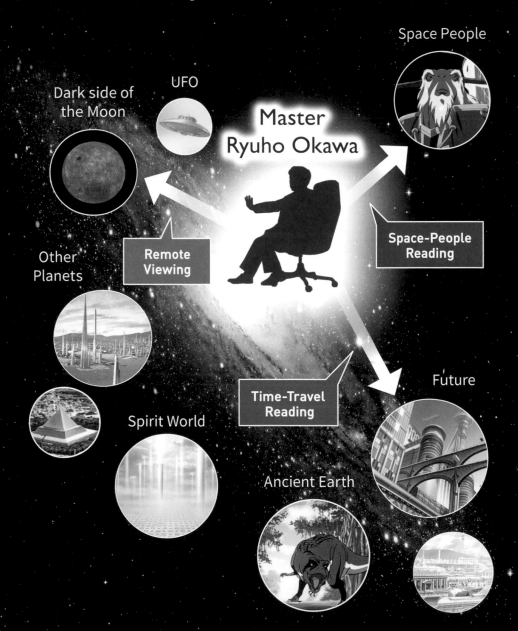

Spiritual Powers
that Transcend Time and Space

UFO Reading

A spiritual ability that makes it possible to talk with the crew inside UFOs that are being filmed or were taken as videos or photos, and to ask them their objectives and other relevant information.

Space-People Reading

The ability to read memories deep inside an earthling's soul, memories that date back thousands or millions of years, and to replay its consciousness from the time it lived as a space person, then engage in a dialog with it. During the conversation, the space person's soul can speak in Japanese by choosing the words it needs from Master Okawa's language center.

Remote Viewing

The ability to send a part of Master Okawa's spirit body to a specified location, such as the dark side of the Moon or the U.S. Air Force base Area 51, to observe the situation there. This is a spiritual power that combines "astral travel" and "spiritual sight," which are two of the Six Divine Supernatural Powers*.

Time-Travel Reading

The ability to spiritually see the past or the future by setting the time and space to be investigated, such as 11th-century Japan or 22nd-century Earth.

*The six divine supernatural powers are *tengen* (spiritual sight), *ten'ni* (spiritual hearing), *tashin* (mind reading), *shukumyo* (fate reading), *jinsoku* (astral travel), and *rojin* (extinction of worldly desires). See Chapter 4 in *The Laws of the Sun* [New York: IRH Press, 2018].

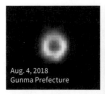

Aug. 4, 2018
Gunma Prefecture

UFO from Planet
Southern in Canis Major

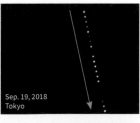

Sep. 19, 2018
Tokyo

UFO from Planet Beta in the Magellanic Clouds. Picture shows the location of the luminous object at 200 seconds and every 10 seconds thereafter from the time it was first recorded.

Ending human rights violations, totalitarianism, and religious suppression by freedom, democracy, and faith

*"We must hammer in the values of freedom, democracy, and faith
in countries such as North Korea, China and
other surrounding nations that are greatly violating human rights,
and create common ground as Earth people
by spreading the teachings that can unite Earth as one."*

From The Laws of Bronze

Through means such as space-people readings, Master Okawa has clearly revealed that behind global conflicts lie influences from space people. The Reptilian-type thinking that says "it's fine to destroy the weak" is prevalent in countries practicing severe violations of human rights, such as North Korea and China. We have learned that there are forces of darkness that are trying to invade Earth and forces of light that are trying to protect it. These facts were only discovered thanks to Master Okawa's Great Enlightenment and his extraordinary spiritual powers.

Master Okawa continues to teach new Buddha's Truths on Earth for the Space Age, so that we can create a world where humankind shares true harmony.

THE PRIMORDIAL BUDDHA
OF THE GREAT UNIVERSE

GOD OF THE EARTH
EL CANTARE

Light Side

Dark Side

Space People Influencing Earth

Defense Force:
Metatron,
Yaidron etc.

Invasive Force:
Ahriman
Kandahar

Faith, Love,
Enlightenment,
Creation of Utopia
to Unite Earth

Materialism and
Atheism to Make
People and the
World Unhappy

Religions

Freedom,
Democracy,
and Faith

Marxism and
Totalitarianism

Politics & Economy

Learning and
Education Based
On Faith

Learning and
Education Based
On Scientism

Learning & Education

Cultural Projects
to Spread the Light

1956 Jul. 7   Born in Kawashima-cho, Oe District (now the city of Yoshinogawa), Tokushima Prefecture

FIRST DEATH

1981 **Mar. 23** **Begins spiritual communication with the heavenly world (Great Enlightenment)**
Joins a major trading house

Jul.   Comes into contact with his branch spirit, Shakyamuni Buddha, who appears before him and reveals the name "El Cantare"

1985 Aug.   Publishes *Spiritual Messages from Nichiren*

SECOND DEATH

1986 **Jul.**   **Resigns from the company and becomes independent**

Late Aug. ~ Sep. 8   *Buddha's Teaching: The Dharma of the Right Mind* and *The Laws of the Sun* (Japanese versions) are written through automatic writing

Oct. 6   Establishes Happy Science and opens up the first office

Nov. 23   Happy Science Launch Commemoration Session—the First Turning of the Wheel of Truth, at Nippori Shuhan Kaikan in Tokyo (currently called Happy Science Commemoration Hall of the First Turning of the Wheel of Truth)

1987 Mar. 8   **The first public lecture: "The Principles of Happiness"** (Ushigome Public Hall)

1991 Mar. 7   **Happy Science is officially approved as a religious corporation**

Jul. 15   The first Celebration of Lord's Descent is held at Tokyo Dome
Lecture: "The Victory of Faith" (El Cantare Declaration)

1994 Jan. 1   **First overseas branch opens in the U.S.**

Sep. 10   **The first Happy Science movie, *The Terrifying Revelations of Nostradamus*, is screened all over Japan**

1995 Mar. 18   Believers voluntarily participate in urgent gatherings and protests in Hibiya and Kameido, Tokyo, demanding investigation into Aum Shinrikyo

1996 Aug. 4   **Head Temple Shoshinkan opens** (General Headquarters moves out)

1997 Apr. 12   The movie, *Love Blows Like the Wind* is screened all over Japan

2000 Oct. 28   The movie, *The Laws of the Sun* is screened all over Japan

2002 Feb. 9   **Success No.1 Buddha's Truth Afterschool Academy opens**

2003 Apr.   **Establishes Senior Plan 21**

Oct. 11   The movie, *The Golden Laws* is screened all over Japan

THIRD DEATH

2004 **May 14** **Experiences a heart attack, is hospitalized the next day, and then a miraculous resurrection**

THE NEW RESURRECTION

2005	Jan. 1	"The Guide for the Mind" begins to be printed in the Japanese Happy Science Monthly starting with the January issue
	Sep. 25	Gives the lecture, "On the Future of Happy Science" at the Memorial Service for Daikokuten (Angels of Wealth)
2006	Jun. 17	**"Never Mind" School for Truancy opens**
	Sep. 30	The movie, *The Laws of Eternity* is screened all over Japan
	Dec. 17	**Hawaii Shoja (first overseas main temple) opens**
2007	Feb. 14	Opening ceremony is held for **Network to Protect Children from Bullying**, an NPO supported by Happy Science
	Mar. 24	Success No.1 Buddha's Truth Afterschool Academy begins to open across Japan
	Apr. 1	**Early childhood education institute, Angel Plan V opens**
	Jun. 26	**Begins missionary tour to branches all over Japan**
	Nov. 18	**Gives the lecture, "Be Positive" (First Turning of the Wheel of Truth Overseas) in the missionary tour to Hawaii Local Branch**
2008	Mar. 21	Gives the lecture, "On Happiness" in the missionary tour to San Francisco Local Temple
	Mar. 23	Gives the lecture, "Happy Attitude" in the missionary tour to Los Angeles Local Temple
	Apr. 1	Future Stars Training Department begins
	Jun. 15	Gives the lecture, "Mind to Believe One Another" in the missionary tour to Seoul Local Temple
	Jul. 27	Gives the lecture, "What is real life?" in the missionary tour to London Local Temple
	Sep. 28	Gives the lecture, "The Way to Success" in the missionary tour to New York Local Temple
	Nov. 9	Gives the lecture, "The Realization of Buddhaland Utopia" in the missionary tour to Taipei Local Temple
2009	Mar. 29	Gives the first lecture at an outside venue overseas, "You Can Be the Person You Want to Become" in the missionary tour to Australia (InterContinental Sydney)
	Apr. 30	**Gives the lecture, "The Manifesto of the Happiness Realization Party"**
	May 25	Holds a press conference for the founding of a political party, The Happiness Realization Party (HRP) Announces 300 candidates in single-member districts and 37 in PR blocks in the 45th House of Representatives election
	Oct. 17	The movie, *The Rebirth of Buddha* is screened all over Japan
	Dec. 7	**An incorporated educational institution, Happy Science Academy is established**

2010	Jan. 1	"Introduction to the Laws of Universe" is recorded (opening of the Dharma gate of The Laws of Universe)
	Mar. 16	"Space-People Reading" is recorded (more recorded hereafter)
	Apr. 1	**Happy Science Academy Junior and Senior High School (Nasu Main Campus) opens** right next to Head Temple Nasu Shoja
	Apr. 3	**Happy Science Institute of Government and Management opens**
	May 16	Brazil Shoshinkan opens
	Aug.	Central Nagasaki Local Temple is constructed, marking the building of 200 local temples
	Nov. 7~14	Gives the lecture, "Love and Work of Angels" (Credicard Hall) and four other lectures in the missionary tour to Brazil
2011	Jan. 7	**New Star Production Co., Ltd. is established**
	Feb. 27~ Mar. 6	Gives the lecture, "The Real Buddha and New Hope" (Kalachakra Maidan, Bodh Gaya) and three other lectures in the missionary tour to India and Nepal
	Apr. 1	"Angel Plan V" begins to open across Japan
	May 21, 22	Gives the lectures, "Love and Spiritual Power" (Ynares Center) and "The Fact and The Truth" (Kowloon Bay International Trade & Exhibition Centre) in the missionary tour to the Philippines and Hong Kong
	Sep. 15~18	Gives the lectures, "Happiness and Prosperity" (Orchard Hotel) and "The Age of Mercy" (Kuala Lumpur Convention Centre) in the missionary tour to Singapore and Malaysia
	Nov. 6	Gives the lecture, "The Power of New Enlightenment" in the missionary tour to Sri Lanka (Waters Edge, Sri Jayawardenepura Kotte)
	Dec. 11	Australia Shoshinkan opens
	Dec. 28	The setting-in-place of the Statue of El Cantare at the prayer hall in Bodh Gaya Main Temple, in Bodh Gaya, India (the first Statue of El Cantare set in place in the Indian subcontinent)
2012	Mar. 17	**The support movement for disabled children, "You Are An Angel!" begins**
	Jun. 2	The first near-future prophecy movie by Happy Science, *The Final Judgement* is screened all over Japan
	Jun. 23	Gives the lecture, "The Light of New Hope" in the missionary tour to Uganda, Africa (Mandela National Stadium)
	Oct. 6	The second near-future prophecy movie, *The Mystical Laws* is screened all over Japan
	Oct. 14	Gives the lecture, "Aspirations for the Future World" in the second missionary tour to Australia (ICC Sydney)
2013	Apr. 1	**Happy Science Academy Junior and Senior High School (Kansai Campus) opens**
2014	Jul. 27	HRP candidate wins a seat in the Oyabe City council election

2015	Apr. 1	**Happy Science University (HSU) opens**
	Jun. 18	"You Are An Angel!" General Incorporated Association is established
	Oct. 10	The movie, *The Laws of the Universe -Part 0-* is screened all over Japan
2016	Jan. 1	The 2,000th book and the 22nd book of the Laws series, *The Laws of Justice* is published
	Mar. 19	The movie, *I'm Fine, My Angel* is screened all over Japan
	Oct. 2	Gives the lecture, "Freedom, Justice, and Happiness" in the missionary tour to New York (Crowne Plaza Times Square Manhattan)
	Nov. 20	**Holy Land El Cantare Seitankan opens**
2017	May 20	The movie, *The World We Live In* is screened all over Japan Wins the Best Feature Film Award at the International New York Film Festival
	May 23	**ARI Production Co., Ltd. is established**
	Aug. 2	Gives the lecture, "The Choice of Humankind" at the Celebration of Lord's Descent (Tokyo Dome)
2018	May 5	The movie, *Heart to Heart* is screened in some theaters Wins the awards: International at Hollywood Verge Film Awards - Best Documentary Feature Film (2019 USA), The IndieFEST Film Awards - Award of Merit (2019 USA), and Canada International Film Festival - Documentary Film - Award of Excellence (2019 Canada)
	May 12	The movie, *Daybreak* is screened all over Japan
	Jul.	"UFO Reading" begins
	Oct. 7	Gives the lecture, "Love for the Future" in the missionary tour to Germany (The Ritz-Carlton, Berlin)
	Oct. 12	The movie, *The Laws of the Universe -Part I-* is released simultaneously in the U.S. and Japan: Wins Best Animated Film Award at Nice International Film Festival and Best International Animation Feature Film Award at London International Motion Picture Awards
2019	Feb. 22	The movie, *The Last White Witch* is screened all over Japan
	Mar. 3	Gives the lecture, "Love Surpasses Hatred" in the missionary tour to Taiwan (Grand Hyatt Taipei)
	Aug. 30	The movie, *Life is Beautiful - Heart to Heart 2 -* is screened in some theaters
	Oct. 6	Gives the lecture, "The Reason We Are Here" in the missionary tour to Canada (The Westin Harbour Castle, Toronto)
	Oct. 18	The movie, *Immortal Hero* is released simultaneously in the U.S., Canada and Japan Wins San Diego International Film Festival - World Premiere Award - Nomination and Madrid International Film Festival - Best Director of a Foreign Language Feature Film
	Oct. 19	"The True Words Spoken By Buddha", the most important sutra was given directly in English

I dedicate my life to the Truth

I wrote "Die for the Truth" and pinned it up in my office.

There are two meanings to those words.
When disciples say they are ready to die for the Truth,
They are expressing the sentiment that they dedicate their
Life and body to Buddha.
And their financial assets too, of course.

When Buddha says that he is ready to die for the Truth,
It means that he dedicates his life and body
To himself and his teachings.

That is why,
I think that I am now engaged in my last fight,
And intentionally live each day thinking,
"Today is my whole life."

I go on missionary tours thinking that
I can die at any time.
I am ready to die for the Truth.
I am putting my life on the line,
So I want you all to do the same.

There is no religion anywhere in the world
That is superior to Happy Science.
The world's best religion should be the world's best.
That is my expectation,
And it shall surely come to pass.
My expectation will surely be realized.
These words will surely be realized.
It may take 10, 20, or 30 years,
But I believe beyond the shadow of a doubt
That Happy Science will become
The world's leading religion.
Don't give up until we are the world's best.
Keep up the fight through generations to come.
This is my message to you all.

From "The Dialogue with Members"
after the lecture in Setagaya Local Temple

ABOUT THE AUTHOR

RYUHO OKAWA was born on July 7th 1956, in Tokushima, Japan. After graduating from the University of Tokyo with a law degree, he joined a Tokyo-based trading house. While working at its New York headquarters, he studied international finance at the Graduate Center of the City University of New York. In 1981, he attained Great Enlightenment and became aware that he is El Cantare with a mission to bring salvation to all of humankind. In 1986 he established Happy Science. It now has members in over 100 countries across the world, with more than 700 local branches and temples as well as 10,000 missionary houses around the world. The total number of lectures has exceeded 3,000 (of more than 150 are in English) and over 2,600 books (of more than 500 are Spiritual Interview Series) have been published, many of which are translated into 31 languages. Many of the books, including *The Laws of the Sun* have become a best seller or a million seller.

Up to date, Happy Science has produced 18 movies. The plan and original story of these projects were given by the executive producer, Ryuho Okawa. Recent movie titles are *Life is Beautiful – Heart to Heart 2 –* (documentary released Aug. 2019), *Immortal Hero* (live-action movie released Oct. 2019), and *The Real Exorcist* (live-action movie to be released in May 2020). He has also composed the lyrics and music of over 100 songs, such as theme songs and featured songs of movies. Moreover, he is the Founder of Happy Science University and Happy Science Academy (Junior and Senior High School), Founder and President of the Happiness Realization Party, Founder and Honorary Headmaster of Happy Science Institute of Government and Management, Founder of IRH Press Co., Ltd., and the Chairperson of New Star Production Co., Ltd. and ARI Production Co., Ltd.

WHAT IS EL CANTARE?

El Cantare means "the Light of the Earth," and is the Supreme God of the Earth who has been guiding humankind since the beginning of Genesis. He is whom Jesus called Father, and His branch spirits, such as Shakyamuni Buddha and Hermes, have descended to Earth many times and helped to flourish many civilizations. To unite various religions and to integrate various fields of study in order to build a new civilization on Earth, a part of the core consciousness has descended to Earth as Master Ryuho Okawa.

El Cantare, the God of the Earth, and His soul siblings whom descended to Earth in the past and flourished many civilizations.

Shakyamuni Buddha

Shakyamuni Buddha (Gautama Siddhartha) was born as a prince into the Shakya Clan in India around 2,600 years ago. When he was 29 years old, he renounced the world and sought enlightenment. He later attained Great Enlightenment and founded Buddhism.

Hermes

In the Greek mythology, Hermes is thought of as one of the 12 Olympian gods, but the spiritual Truth is that he taught the teachings of love and progress around 4,300 years ago that became the origin of the rise of the Western civilization. He is a hero that truly existed.

Ophealis

Ophealis was born in Greece around 6,500 years ago and was the leader who took an expedition to as far as Egypt. He is the God of miracles, prosperity, and arts, and is known as Osiris in the Egyptian mythology.

Rient Arl Croud

Rient Arl Croud was born as a king of the ancient Incan Empire around 7,000 years ago and taught about the mysteries of the mind. In the heavenly world, he is responsible for the interactions that take place between various planets.

Thoth

Thoth was an almighty leader who built the golden age of the Atlantic civilization around 12,000 years ago. In the Egyptian mythology, he is known as God Thoth.

Ra Mu

Ra Mu was a leader who built the golden age of the civilization of Mu around 17,000 years ago. As a religious leader and a politician, he ruled by uniting religion and politics.

ABOUT HAPPY SCIENCE

Happy Science is a global movement that empowers individuals to find purpose and spiritual happiness and to share that happiness with their families, societies, and the world. With more than 12 million members around the world, Happy Science aims to increase awareness of spiritual truths and expand our capacity for love, compassion, and joy so that together we can create the kind of world we all wish to live in.

Activities at Happy Science are based on the Principles of Happiness (Love, Wisdom, Self-Reflection, and Progress). These principles embrace worldwide philosophies and beliefs, transcending boundaries of culture and religions.

Love teaches us to give ourselves freely without expecting anything in return; it encompasses giving, nurturing, and forgiving.

Wisdom leads us to the insights of spiritual truths, and opens us to the true meaning of life and the will of God (the universe, the highest power, Buddha).

Self-Reflection brings a mindful, nonjudgmental lens to our thoughts and actions to help us find our truest selves—the essence of our souls—and deepen our connection to the highest power. It helps us attain a clean and peaceful mind and leads us to the right life path.

Progress emphasizes the positive, dynamic aspects of our spiritual growth—actions we can take to manifest and spread happiness around the world. It's a path that not only expands our soul growth, but also furthers the collective potential of the world we live in.

Programs and Events

The doors of Happy Science are open to all. We offer a variety of programs and events, including self-exploration and self-growth programs, spiritual seminars, meditation and contemplation sessions, study groups, and book events.

Our programs are designed to:
* Deepen your understanding of your purpose and meaning in life
* Improve your relationships and increase your capacity to love unconditionally
* Attain peace of mind, decrease anxiety and stress, and feel positive
* Gain deeper insights and a broader perspective on the world
* Learn how to overcome life's challenges
    ... and much more.

*For more information, visit **happy-science.org**.*

International Seminars

Each year, friends from all over the world join our international seminars, held at our faith centers in Japan. Different programs are offered each year and cover a wide variety of topics, including improving relationships, practicing the Eightfold Path to enlightenment, and loving yourself, to name just a few.

Happy Science Monthly

Happy Science regularly publishes various magazines for readers around the world. The Happy Science Monthly, which now spans over 300 issues, contains Master Okawa's latest lectures, words of wisdom, stories of remarkable life-changing experiences, world news, and much more to guide members and their friends to a happier life. This is available in many other languages, including Portuguese, Spanish, French, German, Chinese, and Korean. Happy Science Basics, on the other hand, is a 'theme-based' booklet made in an easy-to-read style for those new to Happy Science, which is also ideal to give to friends and family. You can pick up the latest issues from Happy Science, subscribe to have them delivered (see our contacts page) or view them online.*

*Online editions of the *Happy Science Monthly* and
Happy Science Basics can be viewed at:
info.happy-science.org/category/magazines/

*For more information, visit **happy-science.org***

OTHER ACTIVITIES

Happy Science does other various activities to provide support for those in need.

- **You Are An Angel!**
  General Incorporated Association
  Happy Science has a volunteer network in Japan that encourages and supports children with disabilities as well as their parents and guardians.

- **Never Mind School for Truancy**
  At 'Never Mind,' we support students who find it very challenging to attend schools in Japan. We also nurture their self-help spirit and power to rebound against obstacles in life based on Master Okawa's teachings and faith.

- **"Prevention against suicide" campaign since 2003**
  A nationwide campaign to reduce suicides; over 20,000 people commit suicide every year in Japan. "The Suicide Prevention Website-Words of Truth for You-" presents spiritual prescriptions for worries such as depression, lost love, extramarital affairs, bullying and work-related problems, thereby saving many lives.

- **Support for anti-bullying campaigns**
  Happy Science provides support for a group of parents and guardians, Network to Protect Children from Bullying, a general incorporated foundation launched in Japan to end bullying, including those that can even be called a criminal offense. So far, the network received more than 5,000 cases and resolved 90% of them.

◆ **The Golden Age Scholarship**
This scholarship is granted to students who can contribute greatly and bring a hopeful future to the world.

◆ **Success No.1**
Buddha's Truth Afterschool Academy
Happy Science has classrooms throughout Japan and in several cities around the world that focus on afterschool education for children. The education focuses on faith and morals in addition to supporting children's school studies.

◆ **Angel Plan V**
For children under the age of kindergarten, Happy Science holds classes for nurturing healthy, positive, and creative boys and girls.

◆ **Future Stars Training Department**
The Future Stars Training Department was founded within the Happy Science Media Division with the goal of nurturing talented individuals to become successful in the performing arts and entertainment industry.

◆ **New Star Production Co., Ltd.**
ARI Production Co., Ltd.
We have companies to nurture actors and actresses, artists, and vocalists. They are also involved in film production.

CONTACT INFORMATION

Happy Science is a worldwide organization with faith centers around the globe. For a comprehensive list of centers, visit the worldwide directory at *happy-science.org*. The following are some of the many Happy Science locations:

UNITED STATES AND CANADA

New York
79 Franklin St., New York, NY 10013
Phone: 212-343-7972
Fax: 212-343-7973
Email: ny@happy-science.org
Website: happyscience-na.org

New Jersey
725 River Rd, #102B, Edgewater, NJ 07020
Phone: 201-313-0127
Fax: 201-313-0120
Email: nj@happy-science.org
Website: happyscience-na.org

Florida
5208 8th St., St. Zephyrhills, FL 33542
Phone: 813-715-0000
Fax: 813-715-0010
Email: florida@happy-science.org
Website: happyscience-na.org

Atlanta
1874 Piedmont Ave., NE Suite 360-C
Atlanta, GA 30324
Phone: 404-892-7770
Email: atlanta@happy-science.org
Website: happyscience-na.org

San Francisco
525 Clinton St.
Redwood City, CA 94062
Phone & Fax: 650-363-2777
Email: sf@happy-science.org
Website: happyscience-na.org

Los Angeles
1590 E. Del Mar Blvd., Pasadena, CA 91106
Phone: 626-395-7775
Fax: 626-395-7776
Email: la@happy-science.org
Website: happyscience-na.org

Orange County
10231 Slater Ave., #204
Fountain Valley, CA 92708
Phone: 714-745-1140
Email: oc@happy-science.org
Website: happyscience-na.org

San Diego
7841 Balboa Ave., Suite #202
San Diego, CA 92111
Phone: 619-381-7615
Fax: 626 395-7776
E-mail: sandiego@happy-science.org
Website: happyscience-na.org

Hawaii
Phone: 808-591-9772
Fax: 808-591-9776
Email: hi@happy-science.org
Website: happyscience-na.org

Kauai
3343 Kanakolu Street, Suite 5, Lihue,
HI 96766, U.S.A.
Phone: 808-822-7007
Fax: 808-822-6007
Email: kauai-hi@happy-science.org
Website: kauai.happyscience-na.org

Toronto

845 The Queensway
Etobicoke ON M8Z 1N6 Canada
Phone: 1-416-901-3747
Email: toronto@happy-science.org
Website: happy-science.ca

Vancouver

#201-2607 East 49th Avenue
Vancouver, BC, V5S 1J9, Canada
Phone: 1-604-437-7735
Fax: 1-604-437-7764
Email: vancouver@happy-science.org
Website: happy-science.ca

INTERNATIONAL

Tokyo

1-6-7 Togoshi, Shinagawa
Tokyo, 142-0041 Japan
Phone: 81-3-6384-5770
Fax: 81-3-6384-5776
Email: tokyo@happy-science.org
Website: happy-science.org

Seoul

74, Sadang-ro 27-gil,
Dongjak-gu, Seoul, Korea
Phone: 82-2-3478-8777
Fax: 82-2-3478-9777
Email: korea@happy-science.org
Website: happyscience-korea.org

London

3 Margaret St.
London,W1W 8RE United Kingdom
Phone: 44-20-7323-9255
Fax: 44-20-7323-9344
Email: eu@happy-science.org
Website: happyscience-uk.org

Taipei

No. 89, Lane 155, Dunhua N. Road
Songshan District, Taipei City 105, Taiwan
Phone: 886-2-2719-9377
Fax: 886-2-2719-5570
Email: taiwan@happy-science.org
Website: happyscience-tw.org

Sydney

516 Pacific Hwy, Lane Cove North,
NSW 2066, Australia
Phone: 61-2-9411-2877
Fax: 61-2-9411-2822
Email: sydney@happy-science.org

Malaysia

No 22A, Block 2, Jalil Link Jalan Jalil Jaya 2, Bukit
Jalil 57000, Kuala Lumpur, Malaysia
Phone: 60-3-8998-7877
Fax: 60-3-8998-7977
Email: malaysia@happy-science.org
Website: happyscience.org.my

Brazil Headquarters

Rua. Domingos de Morais 1154,
Vila Mariana, Sao Paulo, SP
CEP 04009-002, Brazil
Phone: 55-11-5088-3800
Fax: 55-11-5088-3806
Email: sp@happy-science.org
Website: happyscience.com.br

Nepal

Kathmandu Metropolitan City Ward No. 15, Ring
Road, Kimdol,
Sitapaila Kathmandu, Nepal
Phone: 97-714-272931
Email: nepal@happy-science.org

Jundiai

Rua Congo, 447, Jd. Bonfiglioli
Jundiai-CEP, 13207-340
Phone: 55-11-4587-5952
Email: jundiai@happy-science.org

Uganda

Plot 877 Rubaga Road, Kampala
P.O. Box 34130, Kampala, Uganda
Phone: 256-79-3238-002
Email: uganda@happy-science.org
Website: happyscience-uganda.org

ABOUT IRH PRESS USA

IRH Press USA Inc. was founded in 2013 as an affiliated firm of IRH Press Co., Ltd. Based in New York, the press publishes books in various categories including spirituality, religion, and self-improvement and publishes books by Ryuho Okawa, the author of over 100 million books sold worldwide. For more information, visit *okawabooks.com*.

Follow us on:

Facebook: Okawa Books   **Twitter**: Okawa Books
Goodreads: Ryuho Okawa   **Instagram**: OkawaBooks
Pinterest: Okawa Books

Ryuho Okawa's Laws Series

The Laws Series is an annual volume of books that are mainly comprised of Ryuho Okawa's lectures on various topics that highlight principles and guidelines for the activities of Happy Science every year. *The Laws of the Sun*, the first publication of the laws series, ranked in the annual best-selling list in Japan in 1994. Since then, all of the laws series' titles have ranked in the annual best-selling list for more than two decades, setting socio-cultural trends in Japan and around the world.

The Trilogy

The first three volumes of the Laws Series, *The Laws of the Sun*, *The Golden Laws*, and *The Nine Dimensions* make a trilogy that completes the basic framework of the teachings of God's Truths. *The Laws of the Sun* discusses the structure of God's Laws, *The Golden Laws* expounds on the doctrine of time, and *The Nine Dimensions* reveals the nature of space.

The 26th Laws Series

THE LAWS OF STEEL

Living a Life of Resilience, Confidence and Prosperity

The Next 2020 LAWS SERIES *Book*

W hat does it mean to live powerfully and resiliently like *steel*? Learn the way of thinking that will elevate your happiness and make you more prosperous in this book of truth full of wisdom.

THE LAWS OF
STEEL
LIVING A LIFE OF RESILIENCE,
CONFIDENCE AND PROSPERITY
RYUHO OKAWA
AUTHOR OF OVER 100 MILLION BOOKS SOLD WORLDWIDE

Available from March 2020

This book is a compilation of six lectures that Ryuho Okawa gave in 2018 and 2019, each containing passionate messages for us to open a brighter future for ourselves and the world. This powerful and inspiring book will not only show us the ways to achieve true happiness and prosperity, but also the ways to solve many global issues we now face. It presents us with wisdom that is based on a spiritual perspective, and a new design for our future society. With the increasing number of people who read and understand the spiritual truths described in this book, we can overcome different values and create a peaceful world, thereby ushering in a Golden Age.

This book is the lecture in which Master Okawa revealed for the first time about the New Resurrection

ABOUT AN UNSHAKABLE MIND

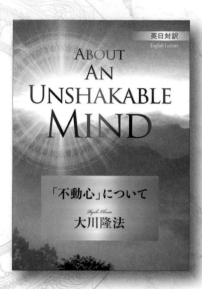

What is the meaning of Master Okawa's 'third death'?

1 The Reason I Could Write An Unshakable Mind at a Young Age
2 My Third Death
3 Great Responsibility
4 The Mission of a Savior

Q1: Building Happy Science Schools All Over the World
Q2: The Name of Our Organization
Q3: Advice On Spreading the Teachings in India
Q4: Keeping Peace of Mind in Bad Economic Situations
Q5: Points to be Conscious of in Local Temple Management
Q6: How to Lead People Who Have Trouble

[This book is available only in local branches and temples. Please refer to the contact information.]

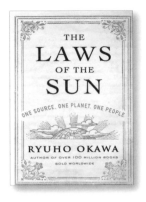

THE LAWS OF THE SUN

One Source, One Planet, One People

Paperback • 288 pages • $15.95
ISBN: 978-1-942125-43-3

In this powerful book, Ryuho Okawa reveals the transcendent nature of consciousness and the secrets of our multidimensional universe and our place in it. By understanding the different stages of love and following the Buddhist Eightfold Path, he believes we can speed up our eternal process of development. *The Laws of the Sun* shows the way to realize true happiness— a happiness that continues from this world through the other.

THE ROYAL ROAD OF LIFE

Beginning Your Path of Inner Peace, Virtue,
and a Life of Purpose

Paperback • 256 pages • $16.95
ISBN: 978-1-942125-53-2

With over 30 years of lectures and teachings spanning diverse topics of faith, self-growth, leadership (and more), Ryuho Okawa presents the profound eastern wisdom that he has cultivated on his approach to life. *The Royal Road of Life* illuminates a path to becoming a person of virtue, whose character and depth will move and inspire others towards the same meaningful destination.

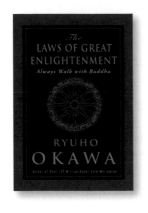

THE LAWS OF GREAT ENLIGHTENMENT

Always Walk with Buddha

Paperback • 232 pages • $17.95
ISBN: 978-1-942125-62-4

Constant self-blame for mistakes, setbacks, or failures and feelings of unforgivingness toward others are hard to overcome. Through the power of enlightenment we can learn to forgive ourselves and others, overcome life's problems, and courageously create a brighter future ourselves. *The Laws of Great Enlightenment* addresses the core problems of life that people often struggle with and offers advice on how to overcome them based on spiritual truths.

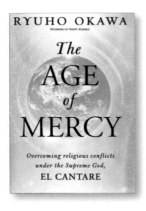

THE AGE OF MERCY

Overcoming religious conflicts under the Supreme God,

El Cantare

Hardcover • 112 pages • $22.95
ISBN: 978-1-943869-51-0

Truth unites the world.

Love ends hatred.

Christians, Muslims, and God-believers

Materialists, communists, and non-believers...

Why do they fight? When will they say, "it's all right"? We bring you the messages of salvation from the Primordial God, Who has been nurturing us humans since the beginning of time. Find the answers you seek in *The Age of Mercy*.

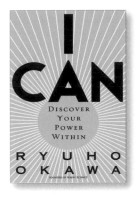

I CAN

Discover Your Power Within

Paperback • 103 pages • $14.95
ISBN: 978-1-937673-25-3

There are countless books on self-development, but none as deep and religious as *I Can -Discover Your Power Within-* by Ryuho Okawa. In this enlightening masterpiece by Okawa, the Master and CEO of Happy Science, you can gain stronger confidence in yourself, overcome adversities and anxieties, and make your dreams come true by learning the spirit of self-help and by knowing the secret to your creative power within. "Saving the poor" is an important idea that leads to world peace, but so are "thoughts have real power," "each person should make effort every day," and "God helps those who help themselves."

LOVE FOR THE FUTURE

Building One World of Freedom and Democracy

Under God's Truth

Paperback • 312 pages • $15.95
ISBN: 978-1-942125-60-0

In this book, Ryuho Okawa shares his personal experiences as examples to show how we can build toughness of the heart, develop richness of the mind, and cultivate the power of perseverance. The strong mind is what we need to rise time and again, and to move forward no matter what difficulties we face in life. This book will inspire and empower you to take courage, develop a mature and cultivated heart, and achieve resilience and hardiness so that you can break through the barriers of your limits and keep winning in the battle of your life.

THE TRUMP SECRET

Seeing Through the Past, Present, and Future

of the New American President

Paperback • 208 pages • $14.95
ISBN: 978-1-942125-22-8

Donald Trump's victory in the 2016 presidential election surprised almost all major vote forecasters who predicted Hillary Clinton's victory. But 10 months earlier, in January 2016, Ryuho Okawa, Global Visionary, a renowned spiritual leader, and international best-selling author, had already foreseen Trump's victory. This book contains a series of lectures and interviews that unveil the secrets to Trump's victory and makes predictions of what will happen under his presidency. This book predicts the coming of a new America that will go through a great transformation from the "red and blue states" to the United States.

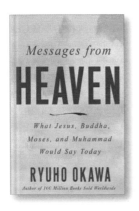

MESSAGES FROM HEAVEN

What Jesus, Buddha, Moses, and Muhammad

Would Say Today

Hardcover • 224 pages • $19.95
ISBN: 978-1-941779-19-4

If you could speak to Jesus, Buddha, Moses, or Muhammad, what would you ask? In this book, Ryuho Okawa shares the spiritual communication he had with these four spirits and the messages they want to share with people living today. The Truths revealed in this book will open your eyes to a level of spiritual awareness, salvation, and happiness that you have never experienced before.

THE LAWS OF INVINCIBLE LEADERSHIP
An Empowering Guide for Continuous and
Lasting Success in Business and in Life

THE STARTING POINT OF HAPPINESS
An Inspiring Guide to Positive Living with Faith, Love, and Courage

INVINCIBLE THINKING
An Essential Guide for a Lifetime of Growth, Success, and Triumph

HEALING FROM WITHIN
Life-Changing Keys to Calm, Spiritual, and Healthy Living

THE UNHAPPINESS SYNDROME
28 Habits of Unhappy People (and How to Change Them)

THE LAWS OF SUCCESS
A Spiritual Guide to Turning Your Hopes Into Reality

THINK BIG!
Be Positive and Be Brave to Achieve Your Dreams

THE MOMENT OF TRUTH
Become a Living Angel Today

CHANGE YOUR LIFE, CHANGE THE WORLD
A Spiritual Guide to Living Now

*For a complete list of books, visit **okawabooks.com**.*